THE
HEALTH
AND
WEALTH
GOSPEL

WHAT'S GOING ON TODAY IN A MOVEMENT THAT HAS SHAPED THE FAITH OF MILLIONS?

BRUCE BARRON

INTERVARSITY PRESS
DOWNERS GROVE, ILLINOIS 60515

InterVarsity Press is the book-publishing division of InterVarsity Christian Fellowship, a student movement active on campus at hundreds of universities, colleges and schools of nursing. For information about local and regional activities, write Public Relations Dept., InterVarsity Christian Fellowship, 6400 Schroeder Rd., P.O. Box 7895, Madison, WI 53707-7895.

Distributed in Canada through InterVarsity Press, 860 Denison St., Unit 3, Markham, Ontario L3R 4H1, Canada.

All Scripture quotations, unless otherwise indicated, are from the Holy Bible, New International Version. Copyright © 1973, 1978, International Bible Society. Used by permission of Zondervan Bible Publishers.

Cover illustration: Roberta Polfus

ISBN 0-87784-327-9

Printed in the United States of America

Library of Congress Cataloging in Publication Data

Barron, Bruce.
    The health and wealth gospel.

    Bibliography: p.
    1. Spiritual healing—United States—Controversial
literature.   2. Wealth—Religious aspects—Christianity.
3. Pentecostalism—United States—History—20th century.
4. United States—Church history—20th century.
I. Title.
BT732.5.B358   1986   277.3'082   86-27503
ISBN 0-87784-327-9

16   15   14   13   12   11   10   9   8   7   6   5   4   3   2   1
99   98   97   96   95   94   93   92   91   90   89   88   87

Acknowledgments

This book benefited from the contributions
of many more people than there is space
here to mention by name. I do wish to thank
specifically, though, those without whose help
the completeness and usefulness of my work
would have been seriously impaired:
Hannelore Bozeman, Mark Butler, Bob
Walker, Ben Byrd, Rockwell Dillaman,
Charles Farah, Gordon Fee, John Gardner,
David Edwin Harrell, Jack High, Jim
Kinnebrew, Robert Kurka, Philip Lochhaas,
Richard Lovelace, Mark Moder, Jayne
Schneider, Vinson Synan, Joni Eareckson
Tada; Jim Hoover, Andy Le Peau, Dan Reid
and Jim Sire, wondrously supportive editors at
InterVarsity Press; and others who have
requested anonymity. The assistance provided
by these people should not necessarily be
taken to imply that they are in full agreement
with my viewpoints.

Special appreciation is due
Robin and Mary Jo, who first encouraged me
to write this book, and to my parents, without
whose training I would have been far from
prepared to write it.

And extra special thanks is due Nancy,
who has contributed to this work not only as
my patient, loving wife but also as constant,
insightful critic and sharpener of all my
thinking and writing.

ONE

First Encounters

I F YOU JUST HAVE FAITH, RITA, GOD WILL ENABLE YOU TO walk."

For Rita, this was no small task. A victim of cerebral palsy, Rita had never been able to walk without leaning heavily on crutches. Since walking was so difficult for her, she spent most of her time in a wheelchair.

I met Rita when both of us were college students. Despite her physical disability, she was looking forward to a life of active Christian ministry and had been accepted by a seminary for the following year. She also knew several friends from a Christian fellowship on campus that taught that bodily healing was among the blessings secured for us by Christ's death.

One night these friends shared their views with her, encouraging her to step out in faith. If she only believed, they said,

God would heal her legs and raise her up from the wheelchair. After they prayed with her, she stood up and walked twenty steps unaided—a personal record—before stumbling.

These fervent Christians exhorted Rita not to lose heart, assuring her that God would manifest a complete healing in the days to come if she would continue to walk in faith. She strove to do just that. But despite her earnest efforts, Rita never again matched her original achievement of twenty unaided steps.

Five days after the initial prayer of faith she called and asked me to visit her. That night we spent several hours seeking to discover and accept what the Lord desired for her and to reinforce her self-image. I was forced to deal with a reality that confronts many ill or physically disabled Christians: the struggle to reconcile their apparently incurable disability with the benevolence of a loving, personal God. Does God want me to stay this way? they wonder. Or does he really want to heal me?

These uncertainties become particularly real and relevant when the handicapped person encounters someone who believes, like Rita's friends from the campus ministry group, that Christians who have faith can be healed of all their physical diseases. This view is the best known of a group of distinctive doctrines being preached by a growing contingent of "faith teachers."

My friendship with Rita brought me face to face with the potential trauma that debilitating physical handicaps offer for faithful Christians. But it was only later, through my wife-to-be, that I began to become aware of the prominence of these "faith teachings" in American Christianity and especially within the branch of Christianity known as the charismatic movement.

Before we were married, Nancy spent six months in a small midwestern town, completing a six-month internship requirement. During her first week there, Nancy was overjoyed to discover two excited, vocal Christians among her coworkers. Her joy subsided somewhat, though, as she began to get to know them. Nancy did not understand when she heard them mutter about ill or less prosperous individuals, "It's too bad they haven't recognized the blessings of Abraham." When she accepted their invitation to listen to a local Bible teacher whom they respected, she heard him criticize Christian ministries of mercy, insisting that instead of just visiting and cheering up the shut-ins and nursing-home residents we ought to lay hands on them in Jesus' name and see these people healed. These teachings were new and unfamiliar to Nancy.

The climax came when *Joni,* the movie chronicling the struggles and spiritual growth of Christian quadriplegic Joni Eareckson Tada, came to town. Nancy, who had seen the movie already, spoke highly of it. Her colleagues, though, did not approve of Joni's ministry. Joni's persistent disability, they explained, demonstrated that she had not yet come to recognize "the whole truth." Not only did they, along with the rest of their church, express no interest in attending the film, but the church placed the following advertisement in the local newspaper, next to the ad for *Joni* on the entertainment page:

NOTICE: We of [name of church] do not believe that it is God's will for man to suffer from sickness, disease or accident, nor do we believe that suffering glorifies God. We believe that God has provided healing through Jesus' scourging and death on the cross.[1]

Experiences with such groups have, at times, made Nancy and me highly skeptical that these teachings have anything to do with the love of God. But then we run into people like Sandy Lewis.

Sandy and her husband were Southern Baptist missionaries for twelve years but were forced to return from the mission field when her diabetes became more serious. In 1978, after eighteen years as a diabetic, she discovered that she had cancer also. On top of that, she had developed a disease in her colon and one in her throat that caused severe coughing spells and made speaking difficult. In short, Sandy was a very sick woman. The prognosis was bleak: continued deterioration.

Then a woman in their church called them and offered to pray with Sandy for healing. The Lewises had not believed in modern healing miracles, but this woman showed them from the Bible why she believed that Christ's death had provided for our physical healing. She and two friends came, prayed over Sandy and declared her healed. When she went back to the hospital, tests revealed no cancer and no excess sugar. All she needed was a skin graft, which was completed successfully on the first try. Except for a few recurrences of symptoms, which she says she has been able to resist by faith, Sandy has had vibrant health ever since.

The Lewises are highly educated, stable Christians, not fanatics likely to believe or fabricate exaggerated claims of miracles. The transformation of their lives and the lives of countless others through divine healing on one hand, and on the other, the cases of intelligent, seemingly reasonable people rejecting all medicine, and dying while claiming to be healed, show most clearly that the faith teachings are too important to be ignored.

Most likely you have heard the faith teachings before, though you may not have recognized them as such. Perhaps you have attended a special seminar broadcast into a friend's church by satellite and have heard Bob Tilton or Norvel Hayes declare that healing is available to all in the audience who will lay hold of it by faith. Perhaps you have heard Marilyn Hickey speak on her radio program about keys to prosperity. Perhaps you have listened to or read materials by another of the well-known leaders of the faith movement, such as Lester Sumrall, Happy Caldwell or John Osteen. Or perhaps you have read about Hobart Freeman, probably the most extreme church leader to be classified as a faith teacher, and the deaths and criminal actions that have ensued since he began to condemn doctors and medicine.

If you are more than vaguely familiar with this contemporary religious phenomenon, you will probably recognize the names of the five faith-teaching ministries that are most prominent across the United States. Generally acclaimed as the faith movement's central figure is Kenneth Hagin, who lives in Tulsa, Oklahoma, and is now in his sixth decade of Christian ministry. He and his son, Ken Jr., have distributed millions of copies of their numerous books, booklets and tapes. Close behind in influence are the husband-wife team of Kenneth and Gloria Copeland of Fort Worth, Texas. They are followed in turn by retired farmer Charles Capps of England, Arkansas; evangelist Jerry Savelle, a former Copeland assistant also based in Fort Worth; and Fred Price, pastor of Crenshaw Christian Center in the Los Angeles area. Since no one can possibly keep up with the proliferation of materials being churned out by many other budding faith pastors and evangelists, this book relies heavily on the work of these five ministries, all of which have regular radio and/or television exposure in major portions of the United States.

Three Main Teachings

The controversies surrounding the faith movement center on three main teachings. We have already noted one of them, divine healing. The second is prosperity—primarily financial prosperity, which faith teachers also view as available to those Christians who are obedient and willing to believe for it.

The third, somewhat less easily explained teaching is commonly known as "positive confession." This is not the traditional Christian practice of confession of sin. Rather, it is a statement, spoken in faith, of what one desires or is requesting from God. God will honor that expression of faith, Hagin and Copeland teach, by fulfilling our desires. To receive healing from physical illness, for example, we should "claim" our healing by praying for it and promptly concluding that we *are* (not *will be*) healed.

Faith teachers stress the value of making this type of confession instead of a "negative confession," or a statement of something we do not desire. They believe that, on making a negative confession, we can open the door to receive unwanted misfortune. For instance, a person who states, "I am sick," upon noticing a sniffle or a feverish temperature can cause those symptoms to turn into a full-fledged illness.

The faith movement has characteristics similar to other teachers and teachings that have gained prominence in twentieth-century America. Their ideas on positive thinking have parallels in renowned pastor and author Norman Vincent Peale and in the ministry of Robert Schuller, pastor of the Crystal Cathedral in California. Their prosperity teaching often sounds much like that of Zig Ziglar, an affluent Texas Baptist and best-selling author of *See You at the Top*. Pat Robertson, founder of the Christian Broadcasting Network, also speaks of keys to prosperity in his best-seller *The Secret Kingdom*. Some have even compared the faith teachers' views on healing to those of Mary Baker Eddy, founder of Christian Science.

Despite these similarities, however, the faith teachings are a distinct, identifiable entity. Of the teachers named in the previous paragraph, only Robertson shares the faith teachers' participation in the form of Christianity known as "charismatic" or "Pentecostal." And Robertson's emphases are noticeably different: he speaks more on the nature of capitalism and the economic system and does not describe the role and nature of faith in the same way as do Hagin, Copeland and their colleagues.[2]

An Important Distinction

Before going any further, I must define the terms *charismatic* and *Pentecostal*. Both words have been used, sometimes interchangeably, in recent years to describe those Christians who believe that the extraordinary gifts (*charismata*, in Greek) described in the Bible by the apostle Paul, such as prophecies, miracle healings and speaking in "tongues" or unknown languages, still exist and should occur in the lives of Christians and in Christian churches today. A church-oriented distinction is commonly made between the two, however, and will be used in this book: *Pentecostal* is normally used to describe those denominations and their members, such as the Assemblies of God and the Church of the Foursquare Gospel, whose roots can be traced back to the outbreak of these spiritual gifts at the beginning of the twentieth century. *Charismatic* generally refers to people who promote these gifts (usually in small groups, but occasionally in worship services) and are part of a movement which sprang up in the late 1950s within non-Pentecostal denominations. It is also used for the many independent churches that believe in tongue-speaking and prophecy but were formed amidst the modern charismatic revival since 1960. The distinction is sometimes vague, but it is useful in separating two movements: on one hand, an early twentieth-century revivalist trend, mostly among lower socioeconomic groups, that did not gain wide-ranging acceptance as a genuine religious practice (Pentecostalism) and, on the other hand, the incredibly powerful charismatic movement, which has left no denomination, geographic region or income group untouched since it began to mushroom twenty-five years ago.

The distinction is an important one, since the teachers and teachings to be examined in this book owe their success largely to their transformation from Pentecostal to charismatic. Formerly a little noticed and seldom respected fringe group, the faith movement has become recognizable enough to be called a "movement," though its adherents and doctrines may not be precisely defined. Since it is not a tightly directed organization and has no official membership, it has gained different names in different areas, further complicating efforts to identify and study it. In some regions churches that support Hagin and Copeland are called "Word" churches because of their insistence that they preach "the uncompromising Word of God."[3] Others call them "word of faith" churches. Some critics, who view the faith message as a man-centered gospel that teaches people to demand whatever they want from God and expect to get it, have sarcastically labeled the movement "name it, claim it." Others have summarized it as the "health and wealth gospel," the "faith-prosperity doctrines," or the "positive confession movement." I will consistently refer to the "faith movement" or "faith message," because these terms seem to be the most widely used, they are broad enough to include all three of the movement's main aspects (healing, prosperity and positive confession) and they do not imply disapproval.

If you have opened this book looking for either an overwhelming affirmation or a damning denunciation of the faith ministries, you have come to the wrong place. I am certainly disturbed by those people who, ignoring the biblical teaching to "test everything" (1 Thess 5:21), swallow every word that proceeds from the mouth of their favorite teacher. But I am equally disturbed by those who, unable to deal calmly with fellow Christians with whom they disagree, unleash vicious diatribes that, even when doctrinally accurate, do more harm than good. Instead, I propose to give a detailed description of the faith teachers and their movement, so as to provide useful data for readers of all persuasions. I will then give a cautious, measured evaluation that—if both sides are willing—will lay the groundwork for meaningful dialog and for resolution of conflict.

Most of us desire a black-and-white world, but the world we live in has many shades of gray. Many find it easy and comforting to conclude that the faith movement is *the* place where God is really working and to jump into it wholeheartedly and with no reservations. Others have sought to prove that the movement is fully and openly heretical; this decision can be equally comforting, for it frees us from having to think about the issues involved and from considering that there might be areas where the faith teachers have more truth than the rest of us. But the comfortable answers, as usual, are not the responsible ones. Just as the wheat and the tares will not be separated until the judgment day, so every person and every theology is a mixture of good and bad. It is time for us to take a discerning but compassionate and open-minded look at a popular belief system which is becoming very influential in American Christianity.

Discernment demands a lot from us. But we will start with a case which, because it is so extreme, is easier to judge.

TWO

A Twist of Faith: The Hobart Freeman Story

S HE WAS A YOUNG CHRISTIAN, IN HER MID-TWENTIES, socially isolated since the recent birth of her first baby. She enjoyed the informal, spirited worship she had discovered a few years earlier, while attending meetings sponsored by the Assemblies of God denomination at her college. But she still yearned for a greater power and fullness in her Christian life. Perhaps, she thought, this other church would meet those needs.

She had visited the church just once, several months back. For some reason she had not returned. But the church began to sound better and better as she learned more about it from members who became customers at her beauty shop near Rockford, Illinois. Those people knew their Bible well, she quickly noticed.

One day a few of the church members came to join her for a coffee break and left some cassette tapes for her to listen to. As she played the tapes, she heard for the first time the teaching that Jesus died on the cross, not only to take the penalty for our sins, but also to provide healing for our bodies. This sounded good to her. Maybe it was the "something more" for which she had been looking.

And so Norma began attending Tuesday evening worship services at Faith Assembly.

She loved it. She found herself surrounded by dynamic, fully committed Christians. The loving relationships that the members shared were easy to see. In short, it was an exciting church and one in which she looked forward to becoming more involved.

As Norma did become involved, she received more tapes to listen to and more books to read. These materials exposed her to new teachings. She frequently heard Romans 12:2 quoted: "Be transformed by the renewing of your mind." The tapes, she was told, were especially valuable in producing this desired "thought reform." She learned that attitudes are more important than circumstances, that it was crucial to keep thinking positively even if difficult circumstances tempted her to feel otherwise. In the area of physical healing, this meant disposing of one's eyeglasses and remaining steadfast in that decision even if the healing did not appear immediately.

At one of the first meetings she attended, Norma heard the group sing, "Christ died in vain if you have a healing you haven't claimed." But she did not become aware of their more extreme teachings on divine healing until much later. She never saw any doctrinal statement from the group, only the flood of tapes and books. Nor did she think that she needed to see a doctrinal statement, for the love and commitment convinced her that she was in the right place.

For Norma the issue of medical science did not assume importance until she became pregnant with her second child. When she expressed her view that she was considering having a doctor present for the birth, she received more tapes and more loving concern from her friends in Faith Assembly. They gave her tapes that covered this very topic, showing why having a doctor involved in delivery—or any other health care—was undesirable. And her best friend within the group told her, "There's no way you can have an evil influence like that in your home." More questions only elicited frowns and disapproval from fellow members, and their attitude grew increasingly painful as she became more attached to the group. Facing childbirth without a doctor was more bearable than hearing her friends call her a compromiser. And she fell in line with what her friends believed.

Gradually but unmistakably, Norma conformed. Since she had been taught not to let herself have negative thoughts, she simply stopped having them, ignoring reality and common sense when necessary. She developed an emotionless, plastic smile. She became uncharacteristically quiet. She experienced the type of sudden behavior changes often associated with mind control.

When she thought about her life outside Faith Assembly, Norma felt an emotional emptiness that resembled an altered state of consciousness. But she had no trouble becoming emotional at Faith Assembly services. There the worship went on for an hour, leaving her and other members in a somewhat mesmerized condition in which suggestibility could begin to take the place of rationality. It was only after this hour that the speaker delivered his message. In such a situation, where her friends around her were uncritical of the speaker's teachings, she had no reason to be otherwise.

As Norma continued to commit herself more deeply to Faith Assembly, she came to share its views of the outside world. She became convinced that the rest of the world was in Satan's power and that it was dangerous to let the world's news fill her mind. Therefore, like most of Faith Assembly's faithful, she stopped listening to radio, watching television or reading newspapers. Instead she devoted this time to daily study of tapes provided by the church. The thought reform that ensued was inevitable, given this exclusive attention to Faith Assembly materials.

Norma's husband, Ronald, showed no interest in becoming part of Faith Assembly. Just as she had been taught, Norma came to believe that he was under Satan's spell. The tapes had warned her to expect Satan to use her family to turn her away from the truth. So when Ronald became angry about Norma's unwillingness to do anything with him or talk about anything other than Faith Assembly, she concluded that he was an instrument of the devil.

Wondering how to regain his wife's respect, one night Ronald demanded that she stay away from a meeting. It did not work. Norma waited for a moment when he was not watching and quietly sneaked out of the house. Ronald heard her leaving and raced after her, but she beat him to the car, locked the doors, and drove away from a desperate, pleading husband.

There seemed no remedy for the shambles of a marriage that had been happy until Faith Assembly entered Norma's life. There she had found something she considered more important, and Ronald's efforts to penetrate her shell were only alienating her further and reinforcing the group's teachings. But her pregnancy was destined to bring matters to a climax. Ronald had flatly rejected her desire to have the baby at home, delivered by him. Twice he made appointments for her to visit a doctor; twice she called to cancel them while he was at work. Neither was willing to budge. Finally, in May, a year after she began attending Faith Assembly and two months before the expected delivery date, Norma moved out and took their young daughter with her.

Ronald managed to find out where she was staying. He drove

to the house and when Norma proved unwilling to leave, he forcibly removed their daughter. During the next few days he tried to pursue legal avenues to force her to deliver her baby in a hospital, but without success. Realizing that his options were very limited, Ronald decided on drastic action: he returned to the home of Norma's friends, lured her into a truck, and immediately drove away with her. They ended up at a relative's house, where they spent the summer.

Having separated Norma from her Faith Assembly colleagues, Ronald eventually succeeded, one week before the baby's due date, in persuading her to give birth in a hospital. After the baby was born he took her on a fishing trip—and arranged to have four experienced deprogrammers waiting for her. In the course of seven days these experts guided Norma in a process of re-education similar to that used with former members of other groups that are more generally recognized as destructive cults. By August, after additional rehabilitation, Norma was able to return permanently to her family. She and Ronald joined a Lutheran church and began accepting invitations to give lectures, teaching others how to avoid the trap of religious groups like Faith Assembly.

The church that had proved so destructive in their lives was unique among the variety of sects that have attracted controversy in recent years. Unlike the great majority of groups accused of cultic practices, Faith Assembly held firmly the central doctrines of orthodox Christianity. Its founder had received all his postgraduate training, including a doctorate in theology, from conservative Christian institutions. He produced a major book on the Old Testament that was published by Moody Press, a well-respected Christian publisher, and earned an award for Christian scholarship.[1] Esteemed early in his career by Southern Baptists and the Church of the Brethren, he later became a teacher of some renown in charismatic circles. But Hobart Freeman's last years of ministry won him nothing but infamy, due primarily to the dozens of deaths that resulted from his teachings on divine healing.

Hobart Freeman and Faith Assembly

Born in a small town in northeast Kentucky in 1920, Hobart Freeman became a Christian in St. Petersburg, Florida, in 1952. He quickly abandoned his career in business to return to school, first at Georgetown College in Kentucky, then at Southern Baptist Theological Seminary in Louisville, and finally at Grace Theological Seminary in Winona Lake, Indiana, where he attained a doctorate in theology. Grace was sufficiently impressed with Freeman's academic and spiritual qualifications to hire him as instructor of Old Testament and Hebrew in 1961. But the school's administrators did not remain impressed for long. As the seminary's president later stated, "It became apparent during the middle of the second year of his employment that his views did not coincide with those of the seminary." Among the issues cited was Freeman's insistence that the holidays of Christmas, Easter and Halloween have pagan origins and thus should not be celebrated by Christians. Freeman also attacked nearly all organized Christian denominations and angered the seminary by starting an independent church in his home.[2]

Grace Seminary's dismissal of Freeman before the end of the 1962-63 school year set in motion his increasing concentration on operating his own independent religious activities. His small church was meeting in a garage in Claypool, Indiana, in 1966 when he (on a trip to Chicago) and later other members of his congregation received the charismatic "baptism in the Holy Spirit." This experience first opened Freeman to the spiritual gifts of prophecy and speaking in tongues. As a result, his teaching and practice began to diverge considerably from what he had learned from the Southern Baptists and Grace Seminary, both of which tend to be very critical of the modern charismatic movement.

Freeman's preference for small, independent house churches rather than denominational bureaucracies left its mark on the form of ministry that arose in his Claypool church. Drawing upon New Testament references to early Christian house churches, Freeman sought to develop a group that thought of the church as a body of believers in which everyone participated in ministry, not as a building where a passive congregation received ministry from a paid clergy. In what may be the earliest reference to Faith Assembly in print, he rejoiced over his degree of success: "It may be difficult for most Christians today to conceive of a church where the pastor is never required to make any 'sick calls' to his members, or does not need to spend long hours counseling them about their problems; but this is the situation which prevails at Faith Assembly (formerly Claypool Church), [because] . . . the members know how to pray for themselves and one another."[3]

Freeman appeared destined for years of inconspicuous ministry as pastor of a tiny, backwoods, unaffiliated church. But Mel Greider, a colorful, reformed alcoholic, apparently was the catalyst for growth in the congregation. His partnership with Freeman saw the church outgrow its garage, and using Freeman's money, Greider remodeled a three-level structure on his property. The building was named the "Glory Barn," and in October 1972 Freeman began five and a half years of preaching at that site.[4]

Although Freeman at first had a relatively respectable congregation, including members of the Full Gospel Business Men's Fellowship International (a large Pentecostal association through which Freeman himself had received "baptism in the Holy Spirit"), his gradual divergence from accepted charismatic teaching began to chase most of the more affluent members away. In their place came economically poorer believers, more comparable in social standing to Pentecostals of the early twentieth century than to the churchgoers who have been touched by the widespread charismatic movement in the last three decades.[5]

Early in 1978, though still attending services in the Glory Barn, Greider was denying "affiliation with any organized religion," including Faith Assembly.[6] Disagreements between him and Freeman were developing—among them Greider's concern over teachings that viewed visiting a doctor as sin. Finally Greider raised the rent to an exorbitant fee, in order to force Freeman to leave. He did. By the end of that year, after several months of holding meetings in a tent, Freeman had erected a new building. Greider returned to alcohol and was dead of a heart attack, at age forty-two, two years later.[7]

A Series of Unnecessary Deaths
In the late 1970s and early 1980s Freeman's influence spread well beyond Indiana. Although accurate assessments are next to impossible, one journalist obtained an estimate that seventeen thousand people, in twenty states and four Canadian provinces, were attending offshoots of this rural midwestern congregation in 1981.[8] And some of these people were following Freeman's teachings wholeheartedly, right to their deaths.

Funeral director Gary Eastlund remembers the first of the cases all too well. It was on Christmas night of 1973 that a young couple arrived at his house with a seven-month-old daughter, victim of a congenital liver defect, dead in the back seat of their car. When the baby had been released from an Indianapolis hospital, as Eastlund reported later, "the parents had been asked to call a doctor if the baby's condition worsened. Instead, the couple called Brother Freeman, who recommended prayer. The couple prayed over the child in their home from about noon on Christmas eve, until about 4 P.M. Christmas day when the baby died."[9]

With the growing avoidance of medicine came also a growing insistence on absolute conformity to the views of the leadership on all issues. Former members report that freedom of thought was permitted in the early years of Faith Assembly but that, as the Indiana church prospered and people struggled for new positions of leadership, those men who adopted "extreme positions of loyalty to Brother Freeman's teachings" won out. In 1979 a group who disagreed with Freeman's definition of faith was rapidly excommunicated after word of their dissent reached the leadership.[10]

Freeman was brashly promoting financial prosperity also, though it was his highly explosive views on healing that grabbed all the attention. As early as 1972 one writer heard him, as guest speaker in a Seattle church, talk about his Cadillac and declare, "My Father is not in the used-car business."[11]

Ironically, Freeman maintained his views on healing and doctors while failing to enjoy the fruits of his own teaching. In his case the disease was visible to all who saw him: polio, suffered when he was a child, forced him to wear a special riser for his withered right leg. According to Faith Assembly's explanation, the healing of this leg "has been claimed by faith, but the manifestation has not occurred yet." An alternate explanation also given was that the limp was an example of " 'Job's trials' designed to enrich [Freeman's] ministry." No one within Faith Assembly ever dared to suggest that Freeman might be guilty of the same lack of faith to which he attributed the illnesses and deaths of his parishioners.[12]

Freeman's newborn grandson died of respiratory failure in February 1980, causing further strain within Faith Assembly and further bizarre reactions from its leaders. Indiana officials claim that a respirator would have saved the baby's life. Freeman, meanwhile, blamed the death on his son-in-law, Bruce Kinsey, for lacking faith. Still, this explanation was potentially damaging to Faith Assembly, since Kinsey was among Freeman's closest associates; it is hard to maintain a ministry's integrity while claiming that one of its primary proponents was so weak in faith as to cause his son to die. So other possible explanations emerged: "though you believed, you might not receive," said some—at least not right away. Or perhaps the dead members of the assembly would later rise and walk the earth in the last days. According to one source, the final verdict was that God was punishing Kinsey for his wild life before he joined the group.[13]

Careless or unguarded teaching usually leads to bizarre behavior when it falls on the ears of fanatically dedicated listeners. The case of Janice Indelicato illustrates vividly the degree of fanaticism that some Faith Assembly branches attained. In 1981, at age forty-one, Indelicato discovered that she had breast cancer. The ministers of her Faith Assembly-affiliated church strictly forbade her to seek medical care. A friend of Indelicato, formerly a member of the same church, recalled later, "They told her that the minute you set foot in a doctor's office, God will abandon you and you'll burn in Hell forever." Indelicato's cancer killed her two years later—unnecessarily, according to the doctor who performed her autopsy.[14]

Perhaps because the fatalities did not occur all at once, but were spread over a number of years, the snowballing tragedy of Faith Assembly went practically unnoticed. Only in May 1983, with the appearance of a series of articles in the *Fort Wayne News-Sentinel,* did the teachings of Hobart Freeman gain national attention. The reporters who prepared the series had documented a dozen Faith Assembly-related deaths through 1977 and an average of about eight per year since then. By the end of 1984 the number of documented, unnecessary deaths had risen to ninety.[15]

Isolated Leadership, Unwholesome Methods
Faith Assembly's teaching became increasingly exclusive, ultimately implying that truly committed servants of God could be found only in Faith Assembly. Freeman's intended meaning

was clear when he preached in 1981, "If [Satan] was permitted to strike at just one church in the state of Indiana, I'll give you one guess which one he'd strike first."[16] As this spiritual elitism took hold, Freeman found ways to distance himself doctrinally from preachers whose teachings most resembled his. He sternly attacked charismatic leaders who had become involved with the so-called shepherding movement, which taught that every Christian should live in voluntary submission to a specific spiritual leader or "shepherd" who provided direct and explicit guidance. (How Freeman's own brand of authoritarianism differed from shepherding is not clear.) Even the other leading exponents of divine healing, preachers with whom Freeman might have been expected to cooperate, received sharp, biting criticism. Very late in his ministry Freeman published *Did Jesus Die Spiritually?* a book undoubtedly aimed at Kenneth Hagin, Kenneth Copeland and other healing preachers who teach that Jesus suffered "spiritual death" as well as physical death on the cross and had to spend three days in hell before being resurrected.[17]

Freeman's method of leading his church differed significantly from normal pastoral behavior. Few of his church members had any contact with him. Not only did he avoid counseling and visitation work, but he even remained out of sight during much of the worship service, entering only after the singing and prayers and quickly disappearing after presenting his message. He carried on an isolated life and kept an unlisted phone number.[18]

Such isolation often fosters self-righteousness and inability to accept correction. Freeman's ministry certainly exhibited these traits. He became angered by constructive criticism even on minor points, bluntly rebuffing those who dared to express disagreement with him. He exuded complete confidence in his accuracy as a prophet of God: "God recently gave a sister a revelation and spoke to her directly and said he's reserved the full faith message for the end time. And [God] went on to say, 'I've revealed the full message to only one man.' I won't say any more because the rest of the revelation is obvious."[19]

With shocking boldness Freeman invoked the terminology of brainwashing to describe the mental reformation that true faith requires. "Developing the habit of positive thinking is . . . practicing thought-control," he wrote. Denying charges that his description of "spiritual brainwashing" embodied nothing more than mental suggestion, Freeman repeatedly quoted from Proverbs 23:7 ("As [a man] thinketh in his heart, so is he"), ignoring the fact that modern translations do not substantiate this King James Version rendering of the passage. "Victorious living," he continued, "is the result of positive thinking and a positive confession." "Everyone *preconditions his life* by what he thinks, believes, and confesses" (emphasis his). "We always receive what we say or confess." Freeman qualified these broad assertions with a reminder that "Jesus never attempted to use faith contrary to the will of God." But this exception was never applied to the issue of divine healing, since Freeman was fully convinced that God had already granted us healing.[20]

Unfortunately, the statistics rebelled against Freeman's advocacy of prayer to the point of excluding doctors. On the contrary, a study of Indiana pregnancy data, initiated after Faith Assembly teachings began to arouse controversy, concluded that pregnant women faced nearly a hundred times the normal danger of death in childbirth between 1975 and 1982 if they were members of Faith Assembly. The perinatal (that is, in late pregnancy or in the first month after birth) mortality rate was almost three times as large for children born to Faith Assembly parents as in the rest of the state.[21]

For many members of Faith Assembly eyesight is the first confrontation with the issue of physical healing. Eyeglasses, worn by millions of Americans who think of themselves as healthy, were classified as medical assistance by Faith Assembly's theology. Some members, after discarding their eyeglasses, have managed to pass their driving tests and have declared themselves healed; but they have still been seen squinting as they read their Bibles. Others have lost their licenses. In several instances members have been spotted driving into the parking lot for a Faith Assembly meeting wearing their glasses but carefully removing them before leaving their cars.[22]

Freeman's very definition of faith could sometimes encourage his followers to ignore reality. Faith, he insisted, is actually more real and accurate than the world our senses perceive: "The very fact that you have faith that God has heard and granted your request is evidence that you have received what you do not yet see." "Jesus," Freeman said, "never sought confirmation of His faith in the visible or sense realm." Rather, Freeman asserted, Jesus accepted the existence of his faith as sufficient evidence that the desired event would come to pass, and we should do the same. "If the sick individual will faithfully confess each day, 'By Jesus' stripes I was healed at Calvary,' his condition and the way that he feels will then begin more and more to conform to what God says about the matter." Freeman cited his own healing from a heart ailment as a personal testimony but avoided mentioning the effects of his polio, from which he was never delivered in thirty-two years as a Christian.[23]

Unlike such teachers as Oral Roberts, who has advocated openness to miracle healing for forty years and has also constructed a major hospital at his university in Tulsa, Freeman insisted that God and medicine could not be reconciled. "To claim healing for the body," he warned, "and then to continue to take medicine is not following our faith with corresponding actions. One should settle the matter beforehand; if we have faith that God will keep His Word and heal us, then we will not need to keep our medicines and remedies around 'just in case.' "[24] Among his evidence was an Old Testament passage (2 Chron 16) in which Asa, an Israelite king, "in his illness did not seek help from the Lord, but only from the physicians." Although the passage implies only that Asa should have sought the Lord as well, Freeman went a step further in inferring that it was wrong to employ the physicians.

Freeman's writings show little tolerance for the skeptic who is not yet convinced of the power of divine healing or the fellow Christian who has sincere theological differences of opinion. Freeman listed, among the main hindrances to effective ministry, "a desire to receive healing through the instrumentality of man"—that is, through medicine. Those guilty of the sin of faithlessness, he noted ominously, "rationalize . . . their doubts and unbelief by contending that God now utilizes the discoveries of medical science, and uses the skills of the doctors and medicines, as well as prayer. This argument has no basis in the Scriptures."[25] If not faithless, Freeman warned, those who reject his teaching are intellectually dishonest: "Those who humbly seek the truth of the validity of this doctrine [that physical healing is guaranteed for all through Christ's death] will see it; those who have prejudged the question in the negative on the basis of their theological background, prejudice, or rational argument, will be unable to receive it."[26]

An observer might expect that the occurrence of unnecessary deaths within Faith Assembly would lead members to question the rejection of medicine. Instead, the group developed a set of beliefs and expectations that made room for such tragedies. No one could prove scientifically that the deaths were not connected to lack of faith. And since this explanation came from leaders of unquestioned authority, the shock of death was neutralized. In addition these adherents had been taught to expect severe testing of their faith. As Freeman wrote: "It is only through trial and tribulation, when the powers of darkness seek to overcome us, that the life and power of Jesus Christ may truly be made manifest in us." More recently Steve Hill, another son-in-law to Freeman, is said to have told followers that "they don't know if they really have faith unless they're in a life-and-death situation, and they have to choose faith or life." Standing firm in the face of death is the greatest and final trial, and the members of Faith Assembly were prepared to face it.[27]

In searching for scriptural support for his direct correlation of faith with health, Freeman sometimes pulled biblical passages out of context, using them in ways that have little resemblance to their original intent. "No one would intentionally invite a doctor," he wrote, "to inject flu germs directly into his bloodstream; and yet this is precisely what you do when you confess that you believe that you are taking the flu at the first symptom, for the Scriptures declare, 'thou art snared with the words of thy mouth' (Prov 6:2)." The passage from Proverbs, however, has nothing to do with positive confession. Rather, in the context, the person snared by the word of his mouth is one who has unwisely pledged to act as surety (guarantor of a debt) for a neighbor.

Freeman's instruction on doubting and negative confession can lead to some almost comical predicaments when people try to communicate their needs and concerns without sounding negative. "Admitting doubt even in a small way will paralyze faith and withhold God's blessings from you," he wrote. "Absolutely refuse to confess doubt, defeat, unbelief, or anything of a negative nature." In that case, how can one tell others that he or she is sick or discouraged and in need of prayer or help? Where possible, of course, believers would simply claim a physical, emotional or financial healing and proceed as if nothing was wrong. But Norma noticed, during her months of attendance at her branch of Faith Assembly, that "I'm overcoming" had become a positive-sounding code word that implied that the speaker had something to overcome. And in one case a family who had no heat or food felt unable to express their need to the church, since that statement would have been a negative confession.[28]

There is, in some sense, a genuinely shared love and concern among the members of Faith Assembly's churches. One couple who watched two sons spend several years under the teachings of Steve Hill recalls having been impressed by the joyful atmosphere when they visited the Rockford, Illinois, church. One of their sons, who was in debt after purchasing a large trailer, received an anonymous gift of $10,000 from someone within the group. This self-sacrifice, though, was reserved for fellow members, as the group tended to discourage normal relationships with outsiders. For instance, that same son, who had formerly sought out friends even in taverns in order to talk and share the Christian gospel with them, began to drop those friendships, explaining, "Those people know where we are; if they want, they can come to us."

Of course, such coldness is never shown to a good prospect. On the contrary, the typical recruitment of a person who seems open to Faith Assembly features the "lovebombing" that Norma experienced. Most recruits are already strong Christians, often with backgrounds in charismatic groups that have aroused in them a yearning for fervent worship, miraculous signs and deeply committed relationships of love. If not already dedicated to a charismatic religious perspective, the proselyte may be a young person displaying the characteristics that have been shown to result in vulnerability to evangelism by any fringe religious group. The father of one Faith Assembly ex-member describes a scenario that researchers, ministers and social workers have heard over and over, from dozens of sects: "Steven [age nineteen at the time] was idealistic, was searching, was away from home for the first time, was having trouble in school . . . and someone came along and tapped him on the shoulder, telling him what a great kid he was and how pleased they were that he was coming to their meetings. Steven was looking for answers to some theological questions that he had, and they said they had the answers, just listen. And Steven did."[29]

But whatever good theology Hobart Freeman and his followers may have taught has been forgotten amidst the ever-growing tragedy of nearly one hundred preventable deaths. As Charles Farah has commented, "If your theology conflicts with the facts, you'd better re-examine your theology."[30]

Freeman never did re-examine his theology. His cold logic left no room for exceptions or special cases, for he was convinced that God had given an absolute promise of healing for our bodies. "There are *no exceptions* to the promises of God," he wrote (emphasis his); "God will fulfill all that He pledged Himself to do, if we meet the conditions."[31] Therefore, if a healing fails to occur, the only available conclusion is that the victim has failed to meet the conditions. Firmly set in its ways, Faith Assembly continues to operate to this day even while its death toll mounts.

It now operates without its founder. Reportedly, Freeman told his followers that he expected never to die. On this point he was indisputably wrong. On 8 December 1984 he died of bronchopneumonia and heart failure, having received no medical treatment for either problem.[32]

Some Constructive Lessons
The pathetic results of Hobart Freeman's ministry do offer a number of constructive lessons that we must learn if we are to avoid similar catastrophes. First, we can see the importance of always keeping our spiritual antennae in operation. Visitors to Faith Assembly churches were often impressed by the worship, which seemed to resemble that of other, reliable charismatic churches; by the noticeable love among the members; and by the apparent commitment to the authority of the Bible. Buoyed by these attractions, many of these visitors became involved without stopping to ask questions about just what the group taught. Only after these people had become thoroughly entangled in the Faith Assembly did they become aware of the fatal

aspects of Freeman's teaching.

If Satan disguises himself as an angel of light (see 2 Cor 11:14), it should not surprise us that he can work within a church too. We must investigate such organizations carefully *before* becoming members. If we discover problems early, it will be relatively easy and painless to leave. If we recognize errors months later, it will be traumatic, if not psychologically impossible, to break from the group. We may already have alienated ourselves from parents, friends and other groups.

Sincere desire to know the truth is not a protection, for the sincerity and devotion of Faith Assembly's members, who came in search of divine direction and believe they have found it, is beyond dispute. The following comment from a couple who followed Freeman's teachings for nine years reveals the nature of this magnetic but disastrous spiritual counterfeit:

> We only want to follow the Lord, but where are you to go for fellowship, who do you trust? You say, fellowship with Christians who teach and follow the Word? Well, that is what we did for nine years. You will not find a Christian group anywhere that studies and adheres to the Word of God as Faith Assembly and its arm ministries.[33]

Having seen so many sincere Christians unwittingly led astray through Freeman's ministry, we must learn to examine with caution seemingly reliable Christian groups.

A second lesson to be learned from the story of Faith Assembly concerns the proper function of miraculous signs and the degree of importance that should be placed on them. The wide international growth of charismatic/Pentecostal Christianity in the twentieth century has produced numerous testimonies to miracles and has encouraged many writers to stress healings, tongues and prophecies as effective, if not essential, tools in winning converts to Christ.[34] These writers find precedents in the wonders worked by Jesus and the apostles and in the attention that these wonders brought to the fledgling Christian gospel. But the men and women of God have no monopoly on miracles. If the ancient Israelites had indiscriminately accepted miracles as authentication of truth, they might have remained submitted to the rule of Pharaoh whose magicians counterfeited Moses' snake and his first two plagues (Ex 7—8). Modern-day spiritualists, through séances and other occult practices, also produce results that seem to defy rational explanation. And recently we have witnessed cases of some preachers, like Jim Jones, whose miracles turned out to be boldly staged. The argument that, if a preacher performs miracles he must be of God, is a faulty and extremely dangerous one.

Third, the accurate and biblical teaching of a preacher today offers no guarantee that he will be accurate and biblical tomorrow. Perhaps no false teacher illustrates this lesson as clearly as Freeman, who seemed to have attained respectability in the evangelical Christian world after publishing his *Introduction to the Old Testament Prophets*. One would have expected that Freeman's ministry would continue to prosper and that those sitting under his teaching would have grown toward spiritual maturity. Instead, following his ministry became a direct path to both spiritual and physical demise. No teacher, however attractive, is exempt from the test of biblical truth.

Fourth, Freeman's case demonstrates that we must not put aside all concern for non-Christian friends once they have made an initial commitment to follow Jesus. Freeman's ministry embraced and misled countless followers who had long ago come to know Christ. Thus it is clear that conversion alone is no safeguard against deception. Moreover, Freeman himself, despite many years of Christian work, became isolated in his own theological sphere and gradually departed from the orbit of orthodoxy. These negative examples display the need for conscientious discipling of new Christians and for meaningful relationships of mutual accountability among mature believers, so that all Christians may be able to stand firm in the faith and train others as they themselves have been trained.

This lesson of building and maintaining accountability among Christians is never more crucial than in situations involving groups, like Faith Assembly, that insulate their members from the rest of the world. When someone comes under the influence of such a group and begins to abandon longtime friends outside the group, those friends often become bitter rather than concerned and increasingly compassionate. Unable to understand the dynamics of the situation and inexperienced in dealing with cultic or authoritarian organizations, these friends (or even parents) lose interest in keeping contact with a former friend who no longer reciprocates for kindness offered. "If she never wants to talk to me, I'm not going to keep calling her," they typically say. But we must realize the bondage in which members of Faith Assembly and many other groups are trapped—a bondage that attempts to sever all of the recruit's contacts with the outside world in order to leave him or her with no alternative to staying in the group. Disillusioned members, having invested all their resources and limited all their socializing to the fellowship, can hardly separate from it successfully unless they have someone on whom to lean for support after they leave. Those of us who are on the outside must strive to keep our hopes up and keep in contact with friends or relatives who are on the inside of such a group.

Similarly, we must resist the temptation to isolate ourselves, whether as individuals or as a group, from other believers. "Church groups need the correction and encouragement of the Christian world at large. A serious imbalance usually tends to amplify within an isolated group of men and women."[35] We should always welcome dialog with other Christians on controversial issues: if we are right, we should want to help our brothers and sisters learn, and if we are wrong, we should desire to be corrected. If we refuse to talk with those who differ with us we will achieve nothing. An opportunity for spiritual growth will be lost.

Among modern faith ministries, Hobart Freeman, exposed as a false teacher by the fruits of his ministry, is the simple case to analyze. No respected Christians will come to his defense. But several other evangelists have attracted large followings and respectability while stressing teachings that are at times strikingly similar to Freeman's. Are Kenneth Hagin, Kenneth and Gloria Copeland, and the other faith teachers preaching falsehoods as potentially fatal as Freeman's have been? Or is their approach to healing, prosperity and positive confession a healthy—or at least harmless—aspect of their message? These teachers are the difficult cases to which we now turn.

THREE

The Roots of the Health & Wealth Gospel

T HE MAY 1983 ISSUE OF KENNETH HAGIN'S MONTHLY *Word of Faith* magazine contains several photographs depicting behavior that many would consider unusual. In two of the photos, men dressed in jackets and ties are performing impromptu dancing in front of a jubilant audience. In another, according to the caption, three adults are shown laughing at the devil. And one of the photos shows a "prophetess" describing a vision she had received.[1]

Such behavior was not unusual among the newly founded Pentecostal churches in the early years of this century. Very few non-Pentecostals would have paid any attention, unless they were interested in heaping ridicule upon the participants.

The people featured in these photos are also of Pentecostal

persuasion—and unashamedly so. Even the participant who reported the events noted that "the services often took unusual turns." But these Pentecostals, unlike their spiritual ancestors two and three generations earlier, are among the leaders of a religious movement that has become increasingly popular in the last fifteen years. The teachings of Hagin and his colleagues—faith, divine healing, prosperity and positive confession—have influenced not just Pentecostals but members of all denominations throughout the United States.

The influence of faith teaching can be illustrated by the comments of a researcher from the Lutheran Church-Missouri Synod, a denomination that has proved most resistent to the inroads of the charismatic movement. "From the correspondence and telephone calls that I receive," he says, "I would estimate that the 'prosperity-healing' doctrines are causing a great deal more confusion, disappointment and tragedy within the Christian Church than the more outlandish cults."[2]

In another telling case, a committee of researchers who spent a year examining Maranatha, a growing and controversial campus ministry organization, made no mention of Maranatha's adherence to these faith teachings. According to one of the committee members, the reason for this omission was the researchers' perception that "there are so many Christians who lean towards those teachings" that to criticize Maranatha on this point would have seriously endangered public acceptance of the whole report.[3]

In contrast to the early Pentecostals, the faith teachers are reaping the benefits of a radically reshaped religious climate. A series of fascinating developments has enabled the faith teachers to emerge from relative obscurity into a position in contemporary Christianity where neither supporters nor detractors can ignore them. By looking at these developments we can gain a perspective on how the faith movement evolved as well as whether its teachings appear to be borne out by history.

European Roots

The story begins in 1828, with modern history's first Pentecostal leader—Edward Irving—a powerful and popular Scottish preacher. His sermons were ranked by many listeners "among the wonders of the time." Irving believed that miracle healings, speaking in tongues and other spectacular gifts "were not exceptional, or for one period alone, but belonged to the Church of all ages, and had only been kept in abeyance by the absence of faith." He suspected that, having been in disuse for so long, these gifts would not reappear until Christ's final return to earth. But in 1830 Mary Campbell, a young, gravely ill Scottish woman, suddenly broke into an unknown language during a prayer time with two friends. A few days later she arose from her bed, declared herself healed, and rapidly became the center of attention. Irving examined the fruits of Mary's experiences and determined them to be genuine. He had been facing increasing disapproval from ecclesiastical leadership anyway, amidst a dispute over whether Jesus could have sinned while on earth, so the danger of public ridicule was no great threat. In November 1831 the spreading phenomenon of ecstatic utterances first penetrated his respectable congregation's Sunday services. Unfortunately, Irving's condemnation by the Church of Scotland, his conviction that the spectacular gifts presaged the end of the world, and the supposed fanaticism inherent in tongue-speaking overshadowed the evidence for several unexpected physical healings. Irving died in 1834, and his movement's success was numerically minimal.[4]

Irving's revival receded into oblivion. But in the midnineteenth century three Christians on the European continent picked up the banner of divine healing while protecting their reputations more successfully than Irving had done. Dorothea Trudel, a Swiss peasant woman unable to offer any medical remedies, began to pray the prayer of faith for invalids. Her results were so shocking that doctors are said to have resorted to false criminal charges in an attempt to curtail her work.[5] A Lutheran minister in Germany, Johann Christian Blumhardt, stumbled into the work of healing in 1842 after parishioners who had heard him preach on faith challenged him to use that faith on a woman whose behavior seemed to reflect demonic possession. A miracle happened, and this humble man became a healer whom even the great theologian Karl Barth could admire.[6] And Swiss pastor Otto Stockmayer earned himself the appellation of "theologian of the doctrine of healing by faith" by promoting a literal interpretation of Isaiah's prophecy that Christ's atonement would take away our "infirmities" (Is 53:4).[7]

The American Connection: Gordon, Simpson and Dowie

The growing renown of these Christian healers inevitably over-flowed into the New World. Their often maligned doctrine took a major step toward respectability in America when Dorothea Trudel's life story fell into the hands of Boston physician Charles Cullis. As director of a tuberculosis sanatorium, Cullis was troubled by the contradiction between the hopeless state of many of his patients and the biblical promise of James 5:15: "The prayer offered in faith will make the sick person well; the Lord will raise him up." Reading about Trudel's marvelous healings only made his internal conflict more intense. He decided to try prayer himself. Anointing a Christian lady afflicted with a severe, painful tumor, he prayed for healing. Shortly after the prayer the woman got up and walked three miles; the tumor gradually disappeared, and the school of faith healing had won a strategic convert.[8]

Cullis was invaluable to the cause of divine healing, not simply because of the authority of his testimony as a doctor but even more so because of his influence on two of the greatest American Christians of his day. Boston was also the home of Adoniram Judson Gordon, widely admired pastor of the Clarendon Street Church from 1869 to 1895. During these years

Gordon became a favorite speaker at revivalist D. L. Moody's Bible institute in Chicago, at Bible prophecy conferences and at various other Christian functions. Along with his preaching mastery and popular insights, Gordon brought with him a strong commitment to divine healing that, though it originated in his own Bible study, was buttressed by his direct contact with Cullis's ongoing ministry of healing.[9]

Gordon popularized his views in *The Ministry of Healing*, which went through many editions. Equipped with a solid academic background, he built a strong case that God still could and did heal miraculously, citing in his defense many witnesses: from early Christian writers like Irenaeus, Origen and Augustine, in addition to recent examples from the mission fields and from personal experience. He cited with approval the work of Stockmayer, who stated firmly that Isaiah 53 promised bodily healing through Christ's atonement. Yet Gordon himself stopped far short of dogmatism, interpreting Isaiah's prophecy and the New Testament connection of it with Jesus (Mt 8:17) with admirable caution:

> In the atonement of Christ there seems to be a foundation laid for faith in bodily healing. Seems—we say, for the passage to which we refer is so profound and unsearchable in its meaning that one would be very careful not to speak dogmatically in regard to it. But it is at least a deep and suggestive truth that we have Christ set before us as the sickness-bearer as well as the sin-bearer of his people.[10]

With similar care Gordon approached the issue of divine sovereignty and its relationship to healing, warning that the doctrine of healing had two sides and that "the acceptance and advocacy of one hemisphere of truth to the rejection of the other" would be heresy. God's will must not be neglected, Gordon wrote, recalling that St. Paul, himself a worker of miracles, had left his colleague Trophimus sick (2 Tim 4:20). Gordon conjectured that God may have kept him ill to protect him from the martyrdom he might have suffered had he remained with Paul. In view of Trophimus's case, Gordon counseled, "If we are told that a brother in the Church is sick let us not make undue haste to declare that he will certainly be restored if we carry his case to God."[11]

In his own body Gordon experienced several unusually quick healings after prayer. In one case, his deliverance from neuralgic spasms, his son later rated the cure "so complete and effectual that the fact of divine intervention can hardly be doubted." But he was not blessed with a painless death—nor would his doctrine have claimed that such was a divine guarantee. His last twelve days of life were racked with delirious insomnia, compounded by a sense of isolation that made his death a relief to his family when it came.[12]

Gordon boldly set forth his belief in Christ's power to heal the body, but always with "caution against dogmatism and pride of opinion in a field where we know only in part."[13] His example of moderation has too seldom been followed.

Charles Cullis was an important supporter on a controversial issue for Gordon. But for A. B. Simpson he was literally a lifesaver. Simpson, raised as a Presbyterian in Ontario, had widened his vision for ministry after his experiences as a pastor in Louisville, Kentucky, had filled him with a burden to reach the world's downtrodden with the gospel. But in 1881, at age thirty-eight, his ministry seemed to have come to an end. Plagued by nervous disorders, this normally superactive man had been reduced to painful, ponderous motion. His physician said that his days were numbered. That summer, vacationing at a resort in Maine, he had the opportunity to attend one of Cullis's meetings, and he heard a series of testimonies to supernatural healing. "It drove me to my Bible," Simpson said later; and in his study he became convinced that healing "was part of Christ's glorious gospel." Shortly afterward, in a secluded forest, he experienced a transforming encounter with God and vowed that as long as he lived he would accept and preach the truth of divine healing and take Jesus—not medicine—for his bodily needs. From those woods he stepped into thirty-five years of uninterrupted health and enormously productive ministry. Cough drops were the closest thing to medicine he touched.[14]

In 1887 Simpson founded what eventually became known as the Christian and Missionary Alliance, the first major movement with physical healing among its basic beliefs. To this day the Alliance's "four-fold gospel" preaches Christ as healer, along with his roles as Savior, sanctifier and coming king. Through this group's rapid growth and his own missionary endeavors, Simpson became, in the words of one biographer, "the greatest exponent of divine healing that the Church has seen in a thousand years."[15] As such, while not preaching against medical science, he clearly intimated that it was not God's ideal means of healing. He encouraged his followers to use human remedies if they were "not ready to trust their bodies fully to the Lord." But in the same breath he affirmed, quoting Isaiah 53, that God " 'took our infirmities,' and He is able to carry them without man's help."[16]

Simpson's main work on the topic, *The Gospel of Healing,* is the product of a man so fervently committed to his theological opinion that he turned almost every conceivably applicable biblical passage into an argument for healing. Along the way he espoused some novel interpretations. "Everything that comes through Christ must come as grace," he argued. "This principle ought to settle the question of using 'means' [i.e., medicine] in connection with faith for healing."[17] One wonders why Simpson, if he considered the human means of medicine as opposed to grace, did not consider the equally human means of evangelistic preaching as opposed to grace! Happily, since he was among the greatest evangelists of his day, his logic did not carry him this far.

Simpson's dramatic vow to the Lord freed him from disease for decades but not forever. During his last few years fatigue began to overtake him and his eyesight faded. In the spring of 1919 he suffered a stroke, but survived half a year longer, slipping into a coma on October 28 and dying the next day.[18]

Like Gordon, Simpson fearlessly preached Christ as healer but kept this message subject to the more important message of Christ as Savior.[19] The third major healing preacher to hit America was not so balanced.

John Alexander Dowie had become a preacher of healing out of desperation. Pastoring a Congregational church near Sydney, Australia, he found himself surrounded by death when an outbreak of bubonic plague struck around 1875. He cried out to God, received a frenzy of inspiration and began praying in faith for his church members. Several dozen of his parishioners had already perished from the plague, but there were reportedly no more deaths after Dowie began to teach and pray for healing.[20]

In 1893 Dowie settled in Chicago where he became, in one historian's words, "the father of healing revivalism in America." By 1900 he had enough money and popularity to purchase a plot of land thirty miles north of Chicago, planning to build his own city. He attracted ten thousand people who moved to "Zion" to live under his fiery leadership.[21]

Divine healing was the focus of much of the controversy that consistently enveloped Dowie's work. He loudly lumped doctors, drugs and devils in the same category and outlawed all three of them in his city. He pointed proudly to the growing collection of crutches in his sanctuary, deposited by the recipients of divine healing. Incredibly dogmatic, he stood firm to his rules even after his daughter burned to death; she died because of disobedience, he said, noting that the fire had started from an alcohol lamp and that alcohol was forbidden in Zion City. But his success was short-lived. In 1906, charged with misuse of funds and with bigamy, Dowie was deposed as Zion's leader. Adding injury to insult, he became physically paralyzed, dying a year later.[22]

Early Pentecostals: Parham, McPherson and Wigglesworth

Despite his eventual fiasco, Dowie nevertheless opened many eyes to divine healing. He laid the groundwork for the building that was to follow. Charles Fox Parham, who had repudiated medicine in 1897 after recovering from heart disease, visited Zion City in 1900. He also examined A. B. Simpson's institute in New York and Frank W. Sandford's Holy Ghost and Us Society in Maine, another fledgling group that believed in divine healing. He learned from these visits, but he was convinced that there was something yet undiscovered. So was Agnes Ozman, one of Parham's students when he opened a Bible school in Topeka, Kansas, in October 1900. Around New Year's Day, 1901, Ozman received the gift of tongues during a period of prayer. Parham, certain that what was missing had now been found, encouraged the group of forty students and seventy-five visitors to seek the gift as well. Most of them obtained it within a few days, and in that nondescript academy the twentieth-century Pentecostal movement was born. In 1906, while Dowie's star was plummeting, William Seymour spearheaded the Azusa Street Revival in Los Angeles. A student of Parham, he was the first to bring significant public attention to the demonstration of the spectacular gifts of the Spirit.[23]

One of these spectacular gifts, of course, is divine healing, and the growing Pentecostal movement meant more visibility for divine healing as well. Ironically, the Pentecostal movement ultimately cast healing in a bad light. It did not take long for Pentecostalism to become equated with fanaticism and emotionalism in the minds of nearly everyone outside the movement. Holiness churches, such as the Church of the Nazarene, that believed in dramatic post-conversion experiences would normally have been somewhat open to faith healing. But they became the Pentecostals' most rabid opponents, both to protect against defections and to distance themselves from the public disdain that the Pentecostal movement was experiencing everywhere. Only the Christian and Missionary Alliance retained healing as a distinctive doctrinal position, and this group gradually became skeptical of the Pentecostal revival as well. Other churches found it much safer to reject categorically everything the Pentecostals stood for. Thus, in a turn of events that would have horrified A. J. Gordon, divine healing disappeared from the mainstream of American Christianity, to be little noticed until after World War 2.[24]

During these years of relative oblivion, healing revivalists continued to cross the country sacrificially offering their services, developing much of the theology that Hagin, Copeland and many others continue to proclaim today (and which will be examined in detail in chapters four and five). Between 1910 and 1947, however, only Aimee Semple McPherson succeeded in shaping a high public profile in the United States. Perhaps this century's most gifted attention-getter, McPherson attracted crowds wherever she went as a traveling evangelist. She continually made headlines after settling in Los Angeles and building the huge Angelus Temple, her church from 1923 until her death in 1944. Though personally ambivalent about faith healing, she found that advertising healing brought bigger crowds, and it appears to have been partly for this reason that she made it a regular part of her ministry. With her mother allegedly screening applicants so as to keep invalids and other severe cases off the stage, "Sister Aimee" began to preach that Christ took two of mankind's curses separately, dying for our sins and being whipped for our sicknesses. Her scandal-filled career kept faith healing in public view but, on the whole, did nothing to enhance its credibility.[25]

The Pentecostal movement did provide a stimulus toward

worldwide ministry for Britisher Smith Wigglesworth, one of the twentieth century's first important ministers of healing. While quietly earning a living as a plumber, Wigglesworth had by age forty-eight invited hundreds to seek salvation or healing as a behind-the-scenes assistant to his wife's preaching work. He had made a private vow not to use medical means. But not until 1907, when he received the Pentecostal "baptism in the Spirit," did he shed his shyness and embark on his own preaching career, which lasted almost to his death at age eighty-seven. "He thought that it was better to die trusting than to live doubting," his son-in-law said of him. And in accord with his convictions Wigglesworth untiringly continued to preach two and three times a day, even through an extraordinarily painful six-year bout with kidney stones. His successes not only in England and the United States, but also in Scandinavia, Australia, New Zealand, Switzerland and even Sri Lanka sowed seeds widely for the message of healing.[26]

Two others from this time period deserve mention, as they have exerted direct influence upon current faith theology. F. F. Bosworth, once the band director in Dowie's Zion church, became a traveling revivalist around 1920 after developing his gift of healing as a pastor in Dallas. In 1924 he wrote *Christ the Healer,* a book that has recently been reprinted (1973) and that Kenneth Hagin has described as one of his personal favorites. In his zeal to present every imaginable theological argument in favor of divine healing, Bosworth, like A. B. Simpson before him, occasionally set forth claims that had little logic behind them. "Why," he challenged his critics, "should not the 'Last Adam' [that is, Christ] take away all that the first Adam brought upon us?"[27] Happily for the sake of his reputation, Bosworth neglected to recall that one of the things the first Adam brought upon us was clothing. But many of his arguments remain as useful to healers and healing advocates in the 1980s as they were to Pentecostals in the 1920s.[28]

The gospel of healing acquired support from a more scholarly writer when T. J. McCrossan published *Bodily Healing and the Atonement* in 1930. Claiming expertise in New Testament Greek, McCrossan frequently buttressed his position by returning to the original Greek text. In another reflection of the continuity of this strand of Pentecostal teaching over the last sixty years, Hagin in 1982 republished McCrossan's book, which had been out of print for half a century. It is now the most scholarly piece of literature in the Hagin ministry's catalog.[29]

Damaging Criticism

Hagin's critics would probably have no more appropriate response to this reprinting than to answer in kind by making available William Edward Biederwolf's book *Whipping-Post Theology* (1934). Biederwolf, a well-educated evangelist alarmed at some of his colleagues' practices, used McPherson, Bosworth and McCrossan as primary examples of the (in his opinion) indefensible view that Christ's atoning death brought us physical healing along with salvation. He wrote a hundred pages refuting these writers and giving his interpretation of the Scriptures he accused them of misusing. Bolstered by personal contact with some former associates of the healing revivalists, he called this form of preaching a "strange perversion of the truth" and wondered if some of them were specializing in healing because it brought larger crowds and better pay than soul-winning.[30]

Biederwolf had plenty of evidence for his concerns. As early as 1906 a Christian author skeptical of faith healing had a clipping from a Philadelphia newspaper in his file, reporting the death from typhoid fever of a two-year-old girl whose parents refused to give her medicine. After his arrest the father identified himself as a member of a "Faith Tabernacle" that believed in prayer as the only means of healing. Such extremes became increasingly common in succeeding decades; Oral Roberts has recalled with gratitude that when he caught tuberculosis as a teen-ager in the 1930s, his father was one of the few Pentecostals around who still believed in doctors.[31]

Perhaps the most damaging evidence against the healers was the result of a committee's investigation of a revival held by Charles S. Price, a McPherson protégé, in Vancouver, British Columbia. The committee followed up on the cases of 350 people who had sought healing during the meetings. It found that, six months later, 39 of the people had died and 301 remained sick. Five claimed lasting healings, but an equal number had gone insane.[32]

Pressures from critics were compounded in the 1930s by Depression economics and schisms within Pentecostalism, so that revival campaigns dwindled for lack of unified, moneyed support. Divine healing had completed the path from semirespectability in 1890 to near total oblivion in 1935, and few would have expected this doctrine ever to reverse the trend and start back up the ladder to success.[33] Even during these lean years, though, the man destined to be the most influential healing teacher of the 1980s was receiving his inspiration.

Kenneth Hagin: Awakening and Ascent

On the morning of August 8, 1934, Kenneth Hagin was halfway through his sixteenth month as an invalid, confined to bed by an incurable heart deformity. He was also halfway through his sixteenth month as a Christian, having been frightened by the specter of death and hell into seeking salvation on April 22, 1933, the very first night of his ordeal. Since then, despite predictions that he could die any day, he had weakly hung on to life. As he read the New Testament, his faith grew to the point where he believed God would raise him from his bed. But still nothing happened as he awoke each morning to another day of boredom and helplessness.[34]

But this morning would be different. For Hagin thought back to the verse that had first sparked his faith: "What things soever ye desire, when ye pray, believe that ye receive them, and ye shall have them" (Mk 11:24 KJV). "The having comes after the believing," he realized. "I've got to believe that my paralysis is gone while I'm still lying here flat on my back and helpless." So he did just that: instead of saying that he *would be* healed, he declared that he *was* healed.[35]

An inner voice said to him, "You believe that you are healed. If you are healed, then you should be up and out of that bed." Tentatively but confidently, he slipped out of bed and cautiously walked once around the bedroom. Two days later he strode to the family breakfast table, miraculously and permanently healed—and spiritually transformed by this evidence of the power of faith in his own life.[36]

Now an exuberant, healthy teen-ager anxious to preach, Hagin got a quick, if inauspicious, beginning when he and a colleague built a makeshift auditorium and conducted revival services in Roland, Texas, eight miles from his hometown of McKinney. Young Kenneth, often lacking any other means of transportation than his feet during these Depression years, wore out four pairs of shoes in a year. But the joy of preaching and serving God overshadowed the inconvenience.[37]

Even though he was a Baptist, Hagin developed contacts with Pentecostals, since he shared their commitment to divine healing. In 1937 he received the "baptism in the Holy Spirit," which in turn caused him to receive "the left foot of fellowship" from the Baptists. Affiliating instead with the Assemblies of God, Hagin pastored a series of churches in the Southwest until 1949, when he began his career as an itinerant evangelist.[38]

"Then he really started climbing," a longtime friend recalled over thirty years later. Actually the climb was long and slow, as Hagin and his family labored under grueling travel demands. But in October 1963 he had enough money and supporters to begin producing books and tapes from an office near Dallas. He moved to Tulsa in 1966, began distributing his *Word of Faith* newsletter in 1968, and was a well-recognized Bible teacher in Pentecostal circles by the early 1970s.[39]

Had it depended on Hagin alone, his ministry probably would have had little impact outside Pentecostalism. However, other events that had been shaping the American religious scene for decades made the blossoming of Hagin's ministry in the late 1960s extraordinarily timely.

Oral Roberts: A Widening Influence

The man most responsible for this shaping was Oral Roberts, whose birth and whose healing followed Hagin's by a year but whose rise to prominence would be unequaled among Pente-costals. Born in northeast Oklahoma in 1918, Roberts was a gifted athlete with visions of a career in politics until, in a high-school basketball game, he suddenly collapsed. Diagnosed as tubercular, he was placed on the waiting list for the local sana-torium. During these weeks of despair, members of his family prevailed upon him first to accept Jesus as his Savior—which he did in February 1935—and then to attend a Pentecostal revival meeting where, Roberts has written, he was healed of both tuberculosis and stuttering. He immediately gave the au-dience a fifteen-minute testimony. Two months later he preached his first sermon.[40]

On the night of his healing, Roberts heard the Lord tell him, "I am going to heal you and you are to take the message of my healing power to your generation."[41] But in the following twelve years of pastoring, teaching and studying he did very little to promote healing. Finally, in 1947, Roberts believed that the time to obey this calling had come. Knowing that he needed "God's anointing to pray for the sick," he entered an extended period of fasting and prayer, approaching God with an urgency that he later described in this way: "I told the Lord I had come to the end of myself and that I would not leave him until he spoke to me." He came out of his prayer closet confident that he had his answer. He promptly put his conviction to the test by renting a large auditorium in Enid, Oklahoma, the town where he was pastoring, and announced a healing service. Over a thousand people came. Roberts's expenses were covered by the offering, and he decided that though "not everyone had been healed . . . a sufficient number had been helped to let me and the people know that God had used me as His instrument."[42]

Roberts went next to Tulsa, where more healings were reported. After that things happened quickly. Before the end of the year he had published his first book, started his own magazine, and taken his ministry on the radio. Aided by banker Lee Braxton, whom he wisely hired as business manager, Roberts rapidly enlarged his resources along with his influence. In his boldest step of all, he went on television in 1954, thrusting the issue of divine healing into an arena where it was sure to draw public attention. Despite inevitable criticism, throughout the 1950s, Roberts's ministry "began to win friends everywhere"— even among governors and senators.[43]

Through the medium of television Roberts reached out to members of non-Pentecostal denominations as no Pentecostal had ever done. Meanwhile he was instrumental in a second key bridge-building venture, the Full Gospel Business Men's Fellowship International (FGBMFI). Roberts, who had conducted businessmen's meetings of his own as early as 1949, became a major supporter of the FGBMFI after his friend Demos Shakarian founded it in 1951. By holding its meetings in hotel ballrooms, this nondenominational organization, while still fully Pentecostal, appealed to middle-class, mainline churchgoers for whom the unrefined ambience of tent revivals was socially off limits. The FGBMFI's "fantastic growth" during the 1950s "marked the acceptance of charismatic religion by thousands of successful middle-class people."[44]

Kathryn Kuhlman: From Scandal to Spotlight

Roberts was the prime emissary of divine healing to the Christian world during the fifties, but Kathryn Kuhlman followed closely behind. Kuhlman, who began her preaching career in 1923, settled down in Denver ten years later after having built up a large following there. Through her program of guest speakers she was exposed to teaching on divine healing, but she herself did not speak on the topic. She might never have done so had events not ruined her ministry and forced her to start over. She and Burroughs Waltrip, a traveling evangelist who spoke in her tabernacle, became romantically involved. He finally divorced his wife to marry Kuhlman in October 1938. The scandal scattered the Denver congregation. The unholy alliance dissolved six years later and Kuhlman was left as an evangelist without an itinerary, her reputation making her morally unacceptable to most pastors.[45]

Somehow her past did not follow her to Franklin, Pennsylvania, a small town north of Pittsburgh, where she began to hold meetings and broadcast a daily radio show in the spring of 1946. A year later, as she was about to begin a sermon on the Holy Spirit, a woman came forward to testify that she had received spontaneous healing from a tumor during the previous night's service—not through specific prayer or laying on of hands or in a healing line (for Kuhlman was not yet doing these things), but in her seat while Kuhlman was preaching. The following week another miracle was reported. By July 1948, when she held her first service in Pittsburgh, her reputation had long preceded her, and she packed an auditorium for two services in one day. She moved to Pittsburgh in 1950, and her ministry of miracles, which eventually broke into television and became one of the CBS network's longest-running programs, was based in that city until her death in 1976.

Kuhlman never wanted to be called a faith healer, and she consciously adopted methods that differed from those seen in most revival meetings. Just after moving to Franklin, while curious but aloof toward divine healing, she quietly drove to Erie to attend a healing evangelist's tent meeting. Her authorized biographer has recorded the disgust she felt that night:

> When the meeting was at the peak of frenzy, a healing line was formed. This line belied the seemingly spontaneous nature of the meeting, for each person who wanted to be in it had previously been assigned a number at the gate. Thus, Kathryn noted with dismay, people had to wait, sometimes for days, to have their number come up. . . . [As the evangelist went down the line] Kathryn could not help but notice that the more seriously ill patients were steered out of the healing line to an "invalids' tent" away from the prying eyes of the public. While some of the people did seem to be genuinely helped—perhaps even healed—the vast majority of those who had broken their crutches had to be helped out of the tent by sympathetic loved ones—still unable to walk. To those the preacher proclaimed that their faith was not strong enough yet.[46]

That experience, combined with the spontaneous nature of the first healings to occur in her own meetings, led her in a somewhat different direction. She never made high-pressure appeals for financial support. She constantly attributed any and all miracles to the power of the Holy Spirit, not to any power within herself. She insisted on medical verification of healings before she would include the stories in her books. Her services were dramatic but not hysterical.[47]

One important result of her approach was unusually generous treatment from the news media, which in turn helped her establish a solid reputation. Early in her ministry, *Redbook* magazine carefully examined the reports of healings and concluded that many of the miracles were genuine. Pittsburgh newspapers often reported on the healings as well. One pastor interested in attracting her to California went to downtown Pittsburgh, asked people at random what they thought of her, and received consistently good reports. All this despite her divorce, her increasing wealth, and the frequency with which members of the audience fainted ("falling under the power," as she termed it) at her services.[48]

As Kuhlman expanded into a nationwide ministry, she transcended denominational barriers just as Roberts had done. But getting approval from individuals in the mainline denominations was one thing. It was another thing altogether to gain the approval of the denominations themselves, which would be needed before the upsurge of Pentecostal practices could become a powerful movement. Shockingly, that is exactly what happened in the 1960s and early 1970s.

Enter: The Charismatic Movement

The tide began to turn with Dennis Bennett, an Episcopal pastor in California who received "baptism in the Spirit" in 1960. When he told his congregation of his experience, his assistant tore off his robes and stalked out of the sanctuary in angry protest. Bennett chose to resign rather than fight, but he was then invited to take over a dying parish in Seattle. Within a few years the charismatic experience overturned and revitalized that church. His celebrated case led to others. Soon there developed a wave of Protestant pastors and leaders exercising Pentecostal gifts. By the mid-1960s charismatic organizations had formed within several of the large denominations.[49]

Then in 1967, in what might be termed the pinnacle of the charismatic movement's amazing achievements, the Catholic Church yielded to this flurry of spiritual excitement. In February of that year a group from Duquesne University in Pittsburgh, seeking a deeper walk with the Lord during a weekend retreat, received the gift of tongues. News of this event, along with the gift itself, quickly spread to influential Catholics at the University of Notre Dame and thence into Michigan and other places in the Midwest.[50]

This time, in contrast to the Pentecostal revival of the beginning of the century, most of the participants in the charismatic renewal continued to function—often with newfound zeal and loyalty—in their traditional denominations. And this time, for most of the denominational leaderships, cautious skepticism turned to guarded acceptance.

The upheaval on the American religious scene meant a golden opportunity for those Pentecostal preachers who could tailor their approach to a wider audience. Some were unable or unwilling to change and thus remained outside the pale of respectability. The primary example in this category was A. A. Allen. Raised in an impoverished, alcoholic family in rural Arkansas, he was introduced to Christianity by Methodists, but he quickly became a Pentecostal evangelist. In his early ministry, Allen later recounted, miracles were seen—but infrequently. After he and his wife examined the situation, they concluded that "the fault had to be within our own lives." So he devoted himself to a prayer vigil until he felt he had broken through into the Lord's presence and discovered the keys to open God's miracle-working power.[51]

In the late 1960s Allen was seen by some as America's most prominent healing revivalist. But while Oral Roberts was coming to terms with the non-Pentecostal world—building a university and joining the Methodist Church—Allen was spitting in its face. He made claims that oil was flowing from people's heads at his meetings, of more and more incredible healings, even of resurrections. Without hesitation he counseled the sick to leave their wheelchairs and throw away their medicines after they had received prayer in the healing line. For those who could not attend one of his meetings, he recommended a handkerchief as a point of contact. Though his mailing list numbered

in the hundreds of thousands, Allen promised individual attention to each request, boasting that "countless thousands are
being healed today by the ministry of blessed cloths."[52]

Regrettably, Allen's own life backed up neither his doctrines
on healing nor his claim that he had found and eliminated the
faults within his own life. The Assemblies of God expelled him
from the denomination after his arrest for drunken driving in
1955. He died in 1970, at age fifty-nine, a victim of acute alco-
holism and fatty infiltration of the liver.[53]

The Hagins Today

It was not the fanatical preachers who would reap the harvest
of the charismatics' newfound respectability. Rather, those who
could *teach* as well as *preach*—who could present themselves in
a manner appealing to the new, more sophisticated charismatics—would be the ones blessed with the most fantastic growth.
As historian David Harrell has pointed out, this was "precisely
the right climate" for Kenneth Hagin, who was "always . . .
more a student and teacher than platform performer."[54] A lis-
tener to Hagin's daily "Faith Seminar of the Air" radio program
will quickly perceive the accuracy of this observation: though
his content is far different, in style and delivery Hagin more
resembles a cultivated, polished Southern Baptist than a Pentecostal.

Since he began producing literature and tapes in the late
1960s, Hagin has had a formidable string of successes. His
monthly newsletter, started in 1971, has seen steady growth in
circulation. In 1974 he (more precisely, his son, Ken Jr., who
serves as his father's right-hand man) founded the Rhema Bible Training Center, where, by the 1980-81 school year, there
were over two thousand students enrolled. The Hagins' correspondence course reported 11,400 students by 1982. Their an-
nual summer Campmeeting has attracted as many as twenty
thousand enthusiasts to Tulsa. In 1981 it was dignified by the

presence of the mayor of Soweto, South Africa. The reports from outside the country have often been just as astonishing— such as the 1,670 pastors who attended a "Rhema World Outreach Seminar" in Costa Rica in 1983. Graduates of the Hagins' school have taken the faith message as far as India and New Guinea.[55]

Kenneth Hagin's influence is certain to be long-lasting, not only because of the large number of believers who have received training through his ministry but also due to his direct effect on nearly every major faith teacher.[56] In fact, Hagin easily outdid the famed Oral Roberts in leaving his mark upon the leading faith preachers of the younger generation, Kenneth and Gloria Copeland.

Kenneth and Gloria Copeland

The Copelands became Christians two weeks apart in the fall of 1962 and received "baptism in the Holy Spirit" three months later. Yet Gloria has written that "for five years we plodded along spiritually without knowing how to use our faith." They were ineffective as Christian servants and remained financially strapped. The clouds did not begin to break until they stepped out in faith in 1967 and moved to Tulsa, where Kenneth enrolled at Oral Roberts University.[57]

Having worked previously as a pilot, he was assigned to Roberts's flight crew, thus earning the chance to travel to healing crusades. By working in the invalid room on meeting nights Kenneth "learned the ministry of praying for the sick from Oral Roberts, an education that only God could have provided."[58]

But according to Gloria, while learning from Roberts was useful, learning from Hagin was far more valuable. It was a Hagin teaching tape, to which the Copelands listened in August 1967, "that revolutionized our lives. . . . We studied and learned from him how to live—to be sustained—by our faith." Kenneth Copeland resolved to devote all his available time to studying

Hagin's materials. He entered the ministry full-time before the end of that year and formed his own evangelistic association in 1968.[59]

Both Copelands, especially Kenneth, have a more dramatic preaching style than their mentor; Kenneth Copeland's striking popularity as a singer illustrates his performing ability. The Copeland ministry has produced few books but a large collection of cassette tapes, presenting largely the same viewpoints as Hagin but with a noticeable accent on financial prosperity. They claim a circulation of 700,000 for their free monthly newsletter.[60]

The Copelands expanded their ministry into radio in 1975, to television in 1979, and to satellite productions in 1981. In addition, they conduct roughly fifteen three- to six-day revival and teaching campaigns each year. Kenneth's specialty in preaching is to teach "how the believers' rights and privileges make it possible . . . to live a victorious and successful life," while Gloria teaches primarily on healing.[61]

The Copelands in turn directly touched another up-and-coming faith teacher, Jerry Savelle, who says that he was "financially broke, spiritually dead, mentally tormented" in 1969 before "a man named Kenneth Copeland came to town and preached the uncompromised Word of God." After defeating his problems, Savelle founded a faith church in Kenya and later served as an associate evangelist with Kenneth Copeland Ministries before forming his own organization, also based in Fort Worth. The two continue to share the podium at various seminars and conferences, but Savelle no longer needs help from bigger names than himself. His ministry reports that it distributes nearly 300,000 copies of his books and tapes each year.[62]

More Faith Teachers

Fred Price, the most prominent Black among the faith teachers, like Copeland credits Hagin with turning his life around. He and his wife, though already Christians, were "in all kinds of trouble going nowhere" until he came in contact with Hagin's ministry and received "baptism in the Holy Spirit" in 1970. They began a church in Los Angeles which grew from 150 members in 1972 to 14,000 in 1985.[63]

Ironically, T. L. Osborn, perhaps the century's most prolific healing preacher in terms of the number of people he has reached, is somewhat less well-known in the United States, because most of his work has been done overseas. In 1947, while toiling as a pastor in Portland, Oregon, Osborn attended a healing revival where he saw the preacher command diseases to leave bodies, exercising the type of faith that Osborn longed for. "When I witnessed this," Osborn has written, "there seemed to be a thousand voices speaking to me at once, all in one accord, saying over and over, 'You can do that!' " Much as Oral Roberts had done, Osborn decided, after a few weeks of improved but still unsatisfying results, to "see no one nor speak to anyone . . . until I had heard from God." He received his answer on the third day, a call to a healing ministry that has continued for forty years.[64]

Most of Osborn's work has been done outside this continent, particularly in Africa, where gigantic crowds and innumerable miracles have been reported. Osborn also has built a large headquarters in Tulsa and maintains contact with the other faith teachers. Yet he remains different in ways other than his choice of mission field. His ministry and materials, for example, do not appear quite as polished as those of Hagin or Copeland. When no others would dare to be associated with the name of A. A. Allen, Osborn assisted Don Stewart, Allen's successor, in establishing his career after his mentor's death in 1970.[65]

The faith message has continued to broaden in the last decade, reaching new sectors of society. Its expansion to university campuses has been facilitated primarily through the work of Bob Weiner, founder of Maranatha Campus Ministries. What began for Weiner as a drug counseling center in Paducah, Kentucky, in 1972 has mushroomed into a ministry that has made its presence known at most of this country's large universities and that, since it holds Sunday morning meetings, could appropriately be termed a student denomination. Maranatha has become best known for its evangelistic boldness, since open-air preaching is its most visible trademark. Its training materials, though, reveal a definite affinity with faith teachings.[66]

It is possible that the most influential faith teacher of the 1990s will be Bob Tilton, who has taken full advantage of the opportunities inherent in this high-technology age. Tilton's Word of Faith Satellite Network, based at his huge church near Dallas, is beaming seminars and revivals into nearly two thousand churches that have hooked up by satellite dishes. Continued growth is almost a certainty as this form of communication becomes more widely affordable. In the spring of 1985 one of his seminars turned into a two-month revival. With healings and miracles being reported across the country, Tilton suddenly captured the spotlight of charismatic Christianity.[67]

Surveying the last one hundred fifty years of teaching on faith healing, we discover that strong faith in divine healing is not an absolute cure-all. The long careers of Hagin, Roberts and Simpson after all three were on the brink of death are cumulatively too impressive to be explained by sheer coincidence. At the same time, it would be ludicrous to accuse such men as Gordon and Simpson of weakening in faith as they approached death. Their physical suffering shows that disease can touch the lives of even these pillars of faith.

Our historical survey also reminds us that divine healing can be preached separately from Pentecostalism, and that in fact many of its most persuasive expositors have had no connection with tongue-speaking or the other gifts now associated with the charismatic movement. This fact should not be surprising, since both Jesus' healings and the apostolic instruction of James 5 make no reference to tongues or prophecy. But this has been obscured by the Pentecostals' prominence in the field of faith healing. It seems that promoters of faith healing would do well to emphasize that healing is not just a Pentecostal doctrine. Tongues and prophecy will always attract suspicions of fanaticism, since most people consider the link between thought and speech a very close one. But the mysteries inherent in the processes of health and sickness force many people to accept the possibility of divine healing.

The Origins of Positive Confession

The history of the faith teachings is primarily a story of the ups and downs of faith healing, for until recently this issue has attracted the attention and controversy. But the modern faith message is more than a message of bodily healing. Where did its other two central themes come from?

The beginnings of positive confession with regard to healing can be spotted as far back as the work of A. B. Simpson, who wrote, "We believe that God is healing before any evidence is given. It is to be believed as a present reality, and then ventured on. We are to act as if it were already true."[68] Why would this well-educated man advocate faith contrary to sensory evidence? Because he believed that the Bible, a higher authority than the senses, teaches healing. Simpson had enough confidence in his interpretation to believe that the prayer of faith would conquer disease, and that if something went wrong our faith would be the most logical place to look for trouble.

This form of teaching naturally led Christians to examine more closely what faith is and how it should be expressed. Among the discoveries was that the Scriptures sometimes view doubt as a mortal enemy to faith. The epistle of James puts it most bluntly: "He who doubts is like a wave of the sea, blown and tossed by the wind. That man should not think he will receive anything from the Lord" (1:6-7). Here lay, it seemed, a scriptural answer to those who had not been healed through prayer and were therefore doubting the promise of divine healing—that very doubt was their undoing. And so began the alliance between the doctrines of healing and positive confession.[69]

The link between positive confession and healing appears in a number of early twentieth-century writings on healing. But the man chiefly responsible for developing and popularizing this idea was E. W. Kenyon. Born in 1868 in New York State, Kenyon received his education in New England, causing some researchers to suspect though no direct connection has been proved, that he was influenced by the mind-science teachings that flourished there in the late nineteenth century. After founding a Bible school in Massachusetts, he moved on to Los Angeles and finally to Seattle, serving as pastor and also preaching over the radio. But his books made the most impact.[70]

Kenyon's writing is full of the pithy statements that typify modern positive confession teaching. "Our faith is measured by our confessions," he forthrightly asserted. "Our confessions rule us." Making a positive confession of God's Word, he wrote, causes the Word to become "a supernatural force" on our behalf, "a dominating force in your lips." "Faith counts the thing done before God has acted. That compels God's action."[71]

The scope of Kenyon's influence has been little short of amazing. Both F. F. Bosworth and T. L. Osborn have freely admitted that they adopted their positive confession teachings directly from Kenyon. Kenneth Hagin also has liberally quoted Kenyon in one of his books, and it has been argued that most of the major ideas advanced by Hagin's ministry came from Kenyon.[72]

Among the currently popular teachers none deserves specific mention more than Charles Capps, who has specialized in exploring the power of spoken confessions. Capps was an Arkansas farmer who, through bad business decisions, had unexpectedly become "so poor I couldn't pay attention." It was then, he reports, that he came across Hagin's book *Right and Wrong Thinking*. The book taught him how to make proper confessions, and his financial downturn was promptly reversed. He embarked on his own teaching ministry in 1973. It is reported that his book *The Tongue, a Creative Force* has sold over 500,000 copies.[73]

The Rise of Prosperity Teachings

Kenyon provided a blueprint for Hagin, Capps and others to follow in the areas of healing and positive confession, but he had no concern for financial prosperity in either his life or doctrine.[74] The development of prosperity teachings is more difficult to trace than the two other pillars of the faith message. Similar ideas have appeared here and there in American religious thought. One hundred fifty years ago Horace Bushnell felt it was the Christian's duty to be prosperous; and at the turn of the century in Philadelphia, Baptist Russell Conwell was famous for his thousands of presentations of the motivating lecture-sermon "Acres of Diamonds." There appear to be no links, though, connecting these men with the Hagin-Copeland version of prosperity teaching.[75]

Hagin states that, even though prosperity was a late addition to his doctrinal system, he learned it from no other human teacher.[76] But it did appear in Pentecostal evangelists whose prominence preceded Hagin's, most notably Oral Roberts.

During his dramatic search for God's direction in 1947, Roberts opened his Bible at random one morning and his eyes fell on 3 John 2: "Beloved, I wish above all things that thou mayest prosper and be in health, even as thy soul prospereth" (KJV). "What I read that morning," Roberts later wrote, "was one of the final touches to the concept of abundant life which has changed the thinking of millions of people." Prosperity thus became an integral part of Roberts's early message. It became even more important when, in seeking funds to go on television in 1954, he introduced the "Blessing-Pact," promising all who contributed $100 to his ministry a refund if they did not receive the gift back from a totally unexpected source within one year. Roberts knew his plan was audacious but firmly believed that this pact "would be the key to unlimited financial blessing for many" of his supporters.[77]

In 1955 Roberts published *God's Formula for Success and Prosperity,* his first book on this topic. By this time, though, A. A. Allen had taken over as the main prosperity preacher among the Pentecostals, repeating the message in half a dozen books and easily surpassing Roberts in brashness as he promised blessings to his contributors. Gordon Lindsay, prolific Pentecostal author and founder of Christ for the Nations Institute in Dallas, chimed in with his book *God's Master Key to Prosperity.* In the 1960s Osborn and Hagin embraced the prosperity message, and countless others have followed since.[78]

This sudden explosion of a previously obscure doctrine begs for explanation. One hypothesis connects the surge in prosperity preaching with the greater demand for funds resulting from nationwide (even worldwide) travel and expensive radio and television programming. It did not take long, of course, for preachers to realize that keys to financial success, like stories of faith healings, attract people who want something more tangible than the brief emotional uplift of a revival meeting. In any case, the adoption of this teaching by Hagin and his colleagues completed the fusion of healing, positive confession and prosperity as the three elements of a major modern religious movement.

As a one-sentence summary, then, the common description of the faith teachings—"you can be healthy and wealthy if you just claim it"—has some substance of truth. If taken seriously, though, it is inaccurate and incomplete. The faith message is more complex and spiritually deeper than many of its detractors seem to have realized. Before passing judgment, we owe the movement—and ourselves—a closer examination of its message and claims to truth.

FOUR

Faith or Fancy?

NOT LONG AGO A RUMOR GOT AROUND THAT THOMAS Harris, author of *I'm OK, You're OK* and founder of transactional analysis, had committed suicide. Somehow this got into the hearing of a prominent American Bible teacher, and then into one of his messages, in which he pointed to Harris's suicide as proof of the bankruptcy of his psychology. Much to his dismay, this teacher discovered that the rumors of Harris's death had been greatly exaggerated. Harris, very much alive, filed a lawsuit for slander and won a considerable out-of-court settlement.

This unfortunate tale illustrates the importance of knowing the facts before speaking or putting pen to paper. In an area as fluid and controversial as the teaching of contemporary evangelists, caution is even more essential. Regrettably, many who are critical of the faith teachers do not reflect an accurate grasp of their teachings. Misinterpretations and partial information abound, leading only to further confusion and dissension between Christians. Some critics have singled out extreme examples which do not represent the movement as a whole.

Before beginning my research for this book I had read a smattering of writings by Hagin and Copeland. In addition I had read about half a dozen books and articles critical of faith teachings. I *assumed* that the critical writings captured the essence of the faith message and its alleged biblical basis. But as I studied the faith teachers' own work, I was surprised to discover how much I did not know. For example, several critics had likened positive confession to Christian Science, but no one had bothered to examine Kenneth Hagin's own explanations of how the two differ.

An accurate analysis of the faith teachings should begin by describing them as objectively as possible, without approval or criticism. To my knowledge, none of the critics of the faith message have attempted to spell out any more than its most central tenets.[1] The faith teachers themselves are not likely to provide an organized summary of their beliefs, as their style is anecdotal and exuberant rather than measured and tightly organized.

This chapter attempts this as yet unattempted systematic survey. But it does not attempt to outline *all* the main emphases of Hagin, Copeland and their colleagues. Many of them coincide with those of evangelical Christianity in general, or at least with the emphases of most of the charismatic movement. The issues surrounding the charismatic movement as a whole have already been discussed in detail by writers of various persuasions[2] and lie outside the scope of this book, as does the even larger question of the truth of Christianity.[3] This chapter tries only to supply a background and an organized approach to show how the faith teachers have developed those beliefs that have been so controversial. Keep in mind that this chapter represents the faith teachers' perspective, not necessarily what this author believes.

Foundations for Faith

Before he sinned, the faith teachers say, Adam lived in a paradisaical world. But by eating of the forbidden tree, Adam died spiritually. He committed high treason and sold out to Satan. God had given him dominion over the earth, but his sin enabled Satan to take over.[4]

God began to redeem for himself a people of his own by making a covenant with Abraham, promising to make him the father of a great nation. Abraham had faith in God and received the promised reward—a child in his old age. Through the period of the Old Testament, God maintained his promise to bless Abraham's descendants, as long as they met the condition of obedience. After leading the Israelites out of Egypt God identified himself to them as Jehovah-Rapha, "the LORD who heals you" (Ex 15:26). In the book of Deuteronomy, speaking through Moses, God repeatedly offered health and wealth as blessings available to those who remained faithful (Deut 7:13-15; 8:18; 28:1-14). God told Joshua, Moses' successor, that if he meditated consistently on the law of Moses he would be prosperous and successful (Josh 1:8). It was because of his covenant with Abraham that God gave Moses the law and these bountiful promises.[5]

The Israelites' repeated failings showed the need for a better covenant between God and man. Having inherited spiritual death from Adam, Israel was inevitably bound to sin.[6] Like all people, Israel needed to have its inward, sinful nature redeemed. Jesus Christ came to earth to be that redemption. Since he took on our sins in order to suffer in our place the penalty for sin, he had to go to hell after his death. Only this "spiritual death" and descent to hell, not just physical death, could provide a sufficient atonement. After he spent three days in hell as our divinely appointed substitute, he was "born again" as God raised him to sit at the right hand of the Father and to serve as our high priest and advocate.[7]

In addition, Jesus' atonement expanded the availability of Abraham's blessing to *all* people. As Paul, inspired by the Holy Spirit, wrote: "Christ redeemed us from the curse of the law . . . in order that the blessing given to Abraham might come to the Gentiles" (Gal 3:13-14). Through Christ, then, we are free from the curses with which the law of Moses threatened any Israelite who failed to follow all the Lord's commands and decrees. Instead we can inherit the blessing of Abraham.[8]

Some critics have misunderstood the faith teachers' view of just what curse Christ has broken. We must not have been freed from the curse, the critics object, for the results of Adam's fall as described in Genesis 3—pain in childbearing, enmity with snakes, and physical death—remain.[9] But the faith message does not claim that the consequences of Adam's fall have passed away. It claims only that our faith can overrule the curse of the *law,* not the curse of the *fall.*[10]

The curse of the law entails three major enemies that believers no longer need to fear: poverty, sickness and spiritual death. All Christians agree, faith teachers would say, that Jesus, in opening the door to salvation, conquered the last of those three foes; fewer realize that he has made the path to physical health and prosperity just as clear.[11]

We become aware of the rights we have in Christ not through sense perceptions—which often suggest that failure is likely—but through "Revelation Knowledge." This kind of knowledge is a profound, heartfelt realization that the promises of Scripture apply to us personally; it produces a recognition of the extent of these promises and a commitment to believe them and act accordingly. When our sensory perceptions seem to contradict revelation truth, we must reject our senses and live by the Word of God.[12]

Healing

One privilege often ignored by Christians, the faith teachers argue, is physical healing. Isaiah 53:4 demonstrates most clearly that Christ's atonement covered bodily healing and that it is always God's will to heal. They maintain that a comparison of this prophecy with other Old Testament passages using the same Hebrew words reveals the best translation to be "Surely our *sicknesses* he hath borne, and our *pains* he hath carried them."[13] Matthew 8:17 removes any doubt as to whether physical or spiritual healing was intended, for Matthew quotes Isaiah 53:4 to show that by healing the physically sick Jesus was fulfilling prophecy.[14]

Those who claim that it is not always God's will to heal contradict themselves by rushing to a doctor when they are sick. If they really believe that God's will is sickness, why should they fight God by seeking medical assistance?[15] Besides, if God did not want to heal everyone, we would expect the gospels to have recorded instances where Jesus turned down requests for healing.[16] Tradition has falsely claimed that Paul's "thorn in the flesh" was a sickness planted by God, say the faith teachers. This thorn, a "messenger of Satan," was probably a person who opposed Paul. It certainly was not a disease.[17] Sickness is of the devil, and Jesus came to destroy the works of the devil.[18]

God intends miracles to be as much a part of the twentieth-century church as they were of the first-century church. Sickness never brings glory to God, but healing does—and miracle healing can be a powerful evangelistic tool. The book of Acts, full of miracles, is a revelation of what God wants the church to be like.[19]

Under the new covenant, the prerequisite to healing is faith. The gospels display unmistakably the role of faith in healing. Two blind men received sight "according to their faith." A woman with a hemorrhage had such faith that she loosed Jesus' power before he knew what had happened. On the other hand, unbelief prevented Jesus from healing in his hometown. When Jesus came to earth as a healer, he demanded faith.[20]

Therefore, the person who meekly asks for healing "if it be thy will" cannot expect results. Such a prayer destroys rather than creates the faith needed for healing. The first step to healing, in contrast, is to know for sure that God's will is to heal. Next we must make sure that we are right with God, free from unbelief or unconfessed sin. Then we can claim our healing in faith.[21]

Some people think that the inevitability of death makes the faith teachers' guarantees of divine healing absurd. As one researcher has said, "There is one illness from which nobody recovers: his last one."[22] But the faith message has incorporated death into its theology, teaching that a person of faith can live a long life (at least seventy years) and then die painlessly. The lives of Christians whose deaths occurred in just this way, among them F. F. Bosworth and E. W. Kenyon, provide experiential evidence to back this view.[23]

Sometimes people who are weak in faith can receive healing through the faith of others, especially if the sick person is a new Christian. Mature Christians, though, must stand on their own faith, for God expects Christians to grow in faith over time.[24] God has bound himself by his Word, the Bible, and can move freely only toward those who are willing to receive by faith. Occasionally God chooses to work a special miracle in a person who does not have the faith, but this is not God's normal procedure.[25]

Among the many reasons why sickness occurs in believers is the lack of knowledge that Jesus' atonement has eternally settled the question of healing for us.[26] Not only the sick person's own ignorance, but also unbelief on the part of the person praying or even the congregation can erect an obstacle to healing.[27] Unwillingness to forgive others can block recovery.[28] And there remain occasions when we simply cannot know why someone was not healed, since God does not always choose to tell us.[29]

Healing can come by a variety of methods. One can simply demand, according to one's rights in Christ, that the sickness leave. Other biblical methods include laying on of hands, anointing with oil, the prayer of agreement by two or more believers and special gifts of healing. Laying on of hands is a valuable recourse for those weak in faith, for it will enable faith to be transmitted from the person praying to the sick person. This process is sometimes described as the Law of Contact and Transmission.[30]

If we are sick, we can receive healing, but God's perfect will is for us not to get sick in the first place. If we remain attentive to God's Word, we will not be sidelined by disease, though the evil one will still try to defeat us. Even Hagin himself, in his fifty years of divine health, has had to battle the devil's attacks: symptoms of illness have come upon him. But he has stood firm in faith and obtained healing before the end of the day each time. This experience should be common for every believer. But very few are fully aware of their rights to claim and maintain permanent health, not just healing from sickness.[31] Going to a doctor is not usually God's perfect will, but it is not a sin; and if we have any uncertainty about whether to see a doctor or stand in faith, we should go to the doctor.[32]

Even though we have claimed healing, the symptoms may not disappear immediately. Sometimes healings take place gradually.[33] Many lose their faith when their senses perceive no immediate results. But we must fix our faith on God's promises, not on our bodily sensations. If we continue to believe that God has given what we have asked for, it will always come to pass.[34] Most people insist that seeing is believing, but those who know the power of faith say instead that believing is seeing.[35] And there is good reason for such faith, for in the mind of God we are already healed. It is not proper to ask him again to heal us, when in fact he has already done it.[36]

Healing is the primary area in which we must affirm revelational truth over sensory perception. But this is not the same as Christian Science. Christian Science denies the reality of pain; Christian faith looks beyond pain to God's promises. Christian Science claims that the power of the mind can bring healing; faith depends on the Word of God to bring healing through the spirit, not the mind.[37]

Positive Confession

Once we obtain healing, the faith movement teaches, we can lose it again if we let doubt replace faith.[38] Instead, in healing as in all other matters of faith, we should confess faith rather than doubt, as exemplified in Mark 11:22-24. In this passage Jesus teaches that a person of faith can speak directly to a mountain and tell it to move. Similarly, we are to speak directly to the mountains in our lives—whether they be physical, spiritual or material problems—and command them to leave.[39] Mark 11:23 tells us that he who truly believes "shall have whatsoever he saith" (KJV); this means that you will have what you say, whether it is *positive* or *negative*. Faith's confessions create realities. Our confessions will either imprison us or set us free.[40]

The role of confession in coming to faith illustrates its role in obtaining other blessings of faith. "It is with your mouth that you confess and are saved" (Rom 10:10). Why should it be different for healing or prosperity? Anything we get from God comes just as salvation comes—through believing with our hearts and confessing with our mouths.[41]

If we are willing and obedient we can write our own ticket with God. We must say what we desire, act on what we have said, receive by faith and confess our faith before others.[42] We do not need to see the results in order to know that God has brought them to pass. Through the steadfast confidence that our faith will bring God's promises to pass, we are entitled to call things that are not as though they were.[43]

The faith involved in a positive confession is different from hope or mental assent. Having a belief that God's Word is true, or a hope that it may come true in our lives some day, will not bring results. Many people pray for healing and walk away saying, "I hope I will get better." This is not faith. Real faith, or "the God-kind of faith," has confidence that the requests made of God have been answered, and it backs up that faith with corresponding actions.[44]

A proper understanding of positive confession also affects our understanding of prayer. When praying for something that is promised by God's Word, such as healing, we need to pray only once. To repeat that prayer denies the Word of God by implying that the first request went unanswered. Instead, we should remind God of what we prayed and thank him for providing the answer.[45]

In intercession for the needs of others, which is a different type of prayer, the laws differ from those that govern the prayer of faith, and repeated supplication is appropriate. The answer to intercessory prayer is not as guaranteed, since the other person's will is involved too. But when we pray for ourselves we can take authority over the devil and consider our needs instantly met.[46] Similarly, we do not need to ask "if it be thy will" in the prayer of faith, where God's will is already clear, but only when seeking God's direction in a prayer of consecration.[47]

A negative confession—that is, a confession of unbelief—can cause an unwanted condition to occur or remain. For example, the person who says, "I'm getting a cold," enables that cold to set in further. Similarly, if someone claims healing but then confesses that symptoms persist, the second confession will nullify the first. Doubt may remain in our heads, since the devil besieges our minds with thoughts of failure, but by remembering the Word of God we can keep doubt out of our hearts. If we resist the devil, he will flee; if we accept fear, the very thing feared will come upon us.[48]

Doubt and fear are the greatest enemies preventing faith from achieving its intended goals. Peter's attempt to walk on water is illustrative: when he began to doubt, he sank. Looking at life's concerns often leads to doubt; looking to Christ's promise never will. We must look at Christ, not at conditions. Admitting doubt is counterproductive. If we feel aches and pains, for instance, we should not broadcast them but should instead reassure inquirers by saying that "Jesus took my infirmities."[49]

Believers who do make the right confessions can still miss out by failing to walk in love. The proper, balanced emphasis on faith will not forget that faith works by love.[50] We must also be feeding continually on the Word of God, since we cannot produce good confessions on the spur of the moment without spiritual preparation.[51]

Positive confession is not capable of getting us absolutely anything and everything. There *are* limits. For example, while many people can "believe for" eighty or a hundred years of healthy life, no one can honestly believe for three hundred years. Some people, who do not have faith for an instant healing, do have the faith to believe that an operation will be successful. God meets these people at their level of faith.[52]

Another limitation is that one must find Scripture to cover the requests we are making. Real faith comes through the Word of God. If we ask for things not promised by the Word, we are guilty of presumption and no longer can be assured of success. If we have the Word behind us, our confession will accomplish what it proclaims.[53]

Prosperity

Positive confession, the faith teachers remind us, is to be used for more than healing. Prosperity, especially financial prosperity, is also available to the believer who appropriates it by faith. Wealth was part of the blessing that Abraham received; poverty was part of the curse that Christ canceled. The New Testament reconfirms God's intent to shower physical, spiritual and material prosperity on Christians. Centuries of tradition have erroneously taught that poverty and holiness go together. But God wants our pocketbooks to prosper along with our spirits. They will do so if, like Joshua, we meditate regularly on God's Word.[54]

The blessing of prosperity also rests on our willingness to meet certain conditions. We must make serving God the top priority in our lives. We must trust God to be our provider. We must stand in faith against all symptoms of lack, just as we stand against all symptoms of disease.[55] Giving to God, by tithes and offerings, is a significant condition for financial prosperity. As we give, we are planting a seed and can trust the Lord to make it bear fruit. Some faith teachers believe that, when we give, we can "believe for" as much as a hundredfold return on our investment.[56]

We should not be satisfied just to get by. Especially those Christians who live in affluent North America should believe for a surplus so as to finance world mission.[57] Besides, God's people were not meant to live on Barely-Get-Along Street.[58]

The promise of prosperity does not free us from trial. In fact, we can expect the devil to attack us all the more as we grow in faith. Serving God can land us in painful situations, much as it landed many of the apostles in jail. But as long as we walk in faith God will deliver and prosper us.[59]

Faith and the "Baptism"

These teachers apply the same principle of faith to the Christian's whole life, including convincing friends and relatives to become Christians, and eliciting obedience from one's children. One area in particular deserves further discussion, for it represents a significant divergence from traditional Pentecostal teaching. The faith teachers affirm, as do most Pentecostals, that all Christians should be baptized in the Holy Spirit subsequent to salvation, and that each person should, at that time, receive the gift of tongues.[60] They differ, however, about the way in which this baptism should be sought, rejecting the opinion that it is often necessary to "tarry," or go through an emotional prayer time that can last several hours. Rather, as in all other things, the believer who prays in faith can count his request as already granted. To receive the Holy Spirit, one must simply ask.[61]

Hagin, as an evangelist, had specialized in enabling "chronic seekers" to receive baptism in the Spirit by faith after they had repeatedly tarried without success. He illustrates the difference between the two approaches with an anecdote that merits repeating. Recalling one instance when two young men answered an altar call and came forward to seek baptism in the Spirit, he describes what happened as four men proceeded to pray with them for forty-five minutes.

There was a church member on each side of one young man. One was hollering, "Hold on, brother, hold on!" The other was hollering, "Turn loose, brother, turn loose!"

A third member was kneeling behind the young man, praying and thumping him on the back like an air-hammer. He was hollering, "Holler louder, brother, holler louder! God will hear you if you'll holler louder!"

A fourth man was in front of the young man, yelling right in his face, and spitting on him every time he opened his mouth. He was hollering, "Give up, brother, give up!"

After forty-five minutes of failure, they all gave up. Hagin then arose and asked the young men, "Do you really want to be filled with the Spirit?" Overcoming their disbelief, he showed them that, instead of shouting to God, they needed simply to receive the Spirit as a gift. Upon hearing that teaching, "Both young men instantly received and started speaking in tongues."[62]

The faith teachers' understanding of baptism in the Spirit

again illustrates their belief in the importance and power of simple, positive faith, whether it be faith for healing, finances, the gift of tongues or for some other need. The best one-sentence summary of what the faith movement stands for comes from Kenneth Hagin, Jr.: "Everything Jesus purchased for us on Calvary can be obtained by faith."[63]

FIVE

Does God Want You Healthy?

NO ASPECT OF THE FAITH TEACHERS' MINISTRY HAS been more controversial than their teaching and practice of healing. It is a topic that regularly attracts wide public attention, media coverage and the trained, critical eyes of researchers. So much has been said and written on this issue that I can hardly begin to cover it. So many arguments have been raised, pro and con, that I can hardly begin to respond to them all. But when we look at the biblical cases for and against divine healing a handful of crucial passages stand out.

By His Wounds We Are Healed

Our primary interest is in three passages which have been understood to teach that there is physical healing in the atonement. In words that have been generally understood to refer to the coming Messiah, the prophet Isaiah writes: "Surely he took up our infirmities and carried our sorrows . . . and by his wounds we are healed" (Is 53:4-5). Portions of this passage are quoted twice in the New Testament: Matthew writes that Jesus' physical healings are a fulfillment of this prophecy (8:17), while Peter cites it in a context of healing from sin (1 Pet 2:24). There has been much perplexity as to just what Christ's sacrifice was intended to cover.

The faith teachers are certain that all three passages have physical healing in mind. Kenneth Hagin states their case with typical confidence: "Isaiah, Matthew, and Peter—three witnesses—tell us that not only did Jesus shed his blood for the remission of our sins, but with His stripes we're healed."[1]

Christians who disagree with this interpretation have responded in a variety of ways. The citation in 1 Peter actually weakens the faith teachers' case, they say, since the passage as a whole has nothing to do with the physical body. Isaiah 53, they point out, also refers predominantly to sin rather than to sickness; the Messiah's sacrifice is connected to his people's iniquities and transgressions a dozen times in the chapter, and the Hebrew words used by Isaiah for "infirmities" and "healed" do not always refer to bodily needs. Matthew interprets Isaiah in this way, but with reference to the healings actually performed by Christ while on earth, not his atoning sacrifice. And Matthew does not quote the Greek version of the Old Testament exactly. Instead, he changes the verb that could mean "vicarious bearing of sickness," to a different one meaning simply "took" or "carried away." Finally, the critics say, if bodily healing were part of the atonement, one would have expected Paul to state this doctrine clearly in his epistles, but he nowhere does so.[2]

These arguments are well constructed and persuasive. Yet, as Keith Bailey has established in his excellent survey of the topic, a number of eminent biblical scholars have espoused an interpretation compatible with the faith teachings. Many of them, including renowned nineteenth-century Old Testament commentator Franz Delitzsch, have specifically argued that Matthew's change of verb was not intended to eliminate the sense of vicarious atonement from the passage.[3]

With such scholars arguing for what the faith teachers affirm instinctively, the complex issue of healing in the atonement cannot be lightly dismissed. Several writers, though, have wisely moved beyond this theological entanglement to a moderating position. They point out that, even if healing is in the atonement, that fact alone does not make healing a universal, immediately available privilege. The faith teachers, in their zeal to appropriate God's promises, sometimes seem to forget this distinction, but it is one that must be made.[4]

Already and Not Yet
The distinction is implicit in the theological use of the terms *already* and *not yet*. We have already been crucified with Christ (Gal 2:20), but we are not yet fully redeemed and still need to renew our spiritual commitment daily. We have already been raised with Christ, and our lives are hidden with Christ in God (Col 3:1-3), but we remain in this fallen world, still waiting for our glorified bodies. We who are in Christ have been freed from the law of sin and death (Rom 8:2) and can be confident of eternal salvation, but we still sin and are not yet experiencing the fullness of redemption. All these examples suggest that there are fruits of the atonement not fully available to us yet. The reality of sick and dying Christians ever since New Testament times suggests that physical healing may sometimes be one of those not-yet benefits.[5]

In defense of the faith teachers, though, it must be said that while they may be exaggerating what is already available to believers, they may still be closer to the truth than those who stress the unavailability of healing. Wade Boggs, Jr., for example, wanting to combat the dualism that sees Satan as a power independent of God, stresses "the inability of Satan to do anything save that which God commanded." In effect Boggs traces suffering back to the all-encompassing will of God, counseling the sick Christian to "turn his thoughts to the power and goodness of God, and ask what good thing God is trying to teach him through this experience."[6] Boggs is right in reminding us of God's ultimate protection, but he appears to have underestimated the consequences of the Fall and the authority granted to Satan in this world. It is hard to preach about the love of God if God is held directly responsible for sickness, let alone natural disasters. "Doctors and research scientists dedicate their lives to the eradication of disease as a dread enemy. The church must not glorify it as a benign friend!"[7]

A look at the writings of Joni Eareckson Tada suggests that though she has given us some magnificent reflections on suffering, the subtle urge to let personal experience become a key to Scripture may work both ways. Just as people who experience miraculous healing often end up believing that everyone should be healed, Tada, after strong faith and prayer made no impact on her quadriplegia, concluded that we should include "if it be your will" in our requests for healing.[8] I don't think that Tada must have done something wrong to impede her healing. But her theological tolerance of sickness may not be in harmony with the attitude of Jesus who repeatedly healed the sick during his earthly ministry.

The Prayer of Faith
Faith teachers have also been criticized for their confident, even demanding approach to prayer for healing. But might not such criticisms hinder a bold exercise of biblical faith? The woman with chronic bleeding, for example, who said "If I only touch his cloak, I will be healed" (Mt 9:21) and dared to touch Jesus even though doing so would have made him (according

to Jewish law) ceremonially unclean, displayed as much boldness as any faith teacher. Yet Jesus applauded her faith; he did
not upbraid her. The Scriptures are full of people who sought
deliverance in similar fashion: Elijah, Esther, David and many
others. God seems to prefer a faith that seeks to change things
rather than a resignation sanctified as submission to God's will.

"Take heart, daughter," Jesus told this hemorrhaging woman, "your faith has healed you." This passage and several others in the gospels show that there is a relationship between
faith and health. Faith teachers have made maximum use of
these passages. Whether we find their view extreme or not, we
must give them, and the world of faith healing in general, credit
for rediscovering a truth that the early church welcomed. Perhaps we are more children of our own scientific age than we
care to admit. Jesus was willing, in episodes like that of the
bleeding woman, to attribute healing to the faith of individuals,
as if he had latent, unlimited power just waiting to be appro-
priated.[9] No Christians today are more eager to receive that
power than those in the faith movement.

Nevertheless, this link between faith and healing must not be
exaggerated. Lindsey Pherigo, who has analyzed the two-dozen
healing stories of Luke's Gospel in search of patterns and common denominators, finds just four references to faith as a factor
in healing—hardly a sufficient basis for asserting that it is always a key precondition. While granting that faith can be a
crucial factor in some instances, Pherigo concludes that "the
process is more mysterious than we can explain, at least at the
present time."[10]

The faith teachers thus run into controversy when they suggest that faith can *always* bring healing. Here is Gloria Copeland's view: "As you study the Word concerning healing, the
force of faith rises up in you to receive God's healing power in
your body." The whole church could be walking in divine
health, she states, were it not for false traditions that have

taught that God does not always heal.[11] Norvel Hayes, in a book in the Hagin ministry's correspondence course, is still more direct in linking lack of healing to lack of faith. Referring to three invalids for whom he prayed at a convention, he reports that one was healed and that "if the other two women would have believed that they were healed that day . . . [they] would be well today."[12]

Biblical Stumbling Blocks
In defending their position, the faith teachers have been unusually careful in explaining 2 Corinthians 12, where Paul describes his battle with a "thorn in the flesh." This has traditionally been interpreted as a physical ailment. By examining the Greek text and drawing comparisons with parallel Old Testament Scriptures, they have given good reasons to doubt that Paul's thorn was a sickness.[13] The disturbing side of their work, though, is that the faith preachers appear to ignore other passages that pose greater threat to the gospel of healing and are less easily explained.

Two references stand out as examples of the illness of godly men: Paul was once sick with an illness that apparently forced him to stop in Galatia (Gal 4:13). This was perhaps an eye problem, since he later wrote to the Galatians that if possible you "would have torn out your eyes and given them to me." Elisha died of an unnamed disease (2 Kings 13:14, 20). Three other passages in Paul's letters provide further evidence along the same line: Timothy's stomach ailment (1 Tim 5:23), the near death of Epaphroditus (Phil 2:30) and the unabated illness of Trophimus (2 Tim 4:20). In all these cases, faithful men of God were sick. The fact that Elisha lived under the old covenant (that is, before Christ) is not relevant, since the faith teachers point to Exodus 15:26 ("I am the Lord who heals you") and Deuteronomy 28 as promises just as good as any in the New Testament.[14] In two of the cases (Timothy and Trophimus),

Paul does not avoid stating that discomfort persists. But the faith teachers seldom refer to these passages.[15]

Those teachers who attribute failure to receive healing to sin or lack of faith on the part of the afflicted sound like the three misguided friends who came to comfort Job amidst his tragedy. Bildad, Zophar and Eliphaz had developed a stern theology which ruled out the possibility of righteous people suffering. Therefore, they concluded that if Job was suffering, he must have done something wrong. And so they spent hours bringing bitter comfort to a man already in great agony by insisting that Job admit to faults he did not have. Little did they know that God had already counted Job as "perfect and blameless" (Job 1:8) or that God's only contention with Job would be for insisting that he, a mere mortal, was entitled to a complete explanation of the purposes behind his suffering. In fact, the three counselors were so far off base in their counsel that God eventually asked Job to pray for *them* so that they might be restored.[16]

When faith teachers follow Job's friends in blaming his sickness on his lack of faith or his supposed negative confession, as some of them do, they seem to be following Job's friends into theological error.[17] But their theology of healing is not so inflexible as it sometimes seems, for it includes a willingness to bend in two major areas: they reserve a place for doctors and medicine, and recognize that healings may not occur instantly.

Medicine: Gift or Temptation?
The Hagins seem well aware of the danger of ruling out medicine, and they distance themselves from the extremes often displayed in early Pentecostalism and most recently by Hobart Freeman. In the June 1983 *Word of Faith* magazine, the first issue printed after the Fort Wayne newspaper articles brought national attention to Freeman's fatal doctrines, Hagin declared that, although he had been blessed with divine health for half

a century, he did not oppose medical science. "I believe in good doctors, especially Christian doctors," he asserted. "And if I needed a doctor, I'd go to one. . . . In recent years, I've sent some people to the doctor and paid their bill myself. I've even bought medicine for them, because I realized they needed to go."[18]

The faith teachers unanimously support the use of doctors. Yet sometimes in the same breath they seem to suggest that doctors should serve only as a stopgap measure for Christians until they reach a higher level of faith. The younger Hagin recalls that his father might have died without medical care but adds that the doctors could only keep him in a stable condition until the faith of God worked in his heart. "Take [medicine]," he writes, "until you can get enough faith in you to where you don't have to take it." Gloria Copeland concurs: "Divine healing without any outside help—doctors or medicine—is God's best but many are not able to receive by faith alone. Until you are able to live in divine health, go to the doctor in faith."[19] This view raises a question: how do we decide when we have enough faith to "live in divine health" and stop taking medicine? Not until we are healed? Or can "real faith" sometimes require giving up medicine when serious symptoms persist? If the latter is the case, the Hagins and Copelands, despite their tolerance of doctors, remain open to the danger that their followers, by shunning medical care at the wrong time, might die of an untreated illness.

The same ambiguity appears in Fred Price, who shares the conviction that medicine is neither sinful nor ideal. He repeatedly stresses that, until one has obtained the physical manifestation of a healing, it is unwise to dispense with medical assistance. "I have watched people die" that way, he warns.[20] Yet at the same time he also intimates that strong faith makes other remedies superfluous. "When you have developed your faith to such an extent that you can stand on the promises of God, then you won't need medicine," he states. While it is "not opposed to divine healing," human medicine, in Price's view, is "on a lower level."[21]

We see then that faith teachers respect the field of medicine and, commendably, have made statements designed to avert the tragedies that ensue when rash presumption replaces faith. Yet, by establishing divine healing as superior to medical healing, they may unintentionally be encouraging the very behavior they have warned against. If strong faith makes medicine unnecessary, then anyone who needs medicine does not have strong faith. In a church that holds the views of Hagin and Price it would be easy to equate acceptance of medical aid with weakness. In that case subtle peer pressure could compel the sick to claim their healing and receive admiration for their faith rather than go to the doctor and risk implicit disapproval. The choice a person makes depends largely on whether that individual has been influenced by "Keep taking your medicine until your healing is manifested" or by "If your faith is strong enough you don't need medicine."

Even if open to ambiguous interpretation, the faith teachers' acceptance of doctors softens their doctrine of healing. So does their admission that healing may not appear instantly, even if a sick person acts in faith and meets all the conditions. This second qualification, which they stress frequently,[22] is not surprising. All Christian healers must deal with the reality that many for whom they pray do not appear to be healed. To deny that Christ's atonement has guaranteed our healing would remove the foundation from their ministry and, as they see it, would be untrue to the Scriptures. But to blame every seemingly unanswered prayer for healing on the sick person's faithlessness would eventually undermine the movement's credibility. (In some cases it could also backfire on a preacher. Imagine Hobart Freeman trying to retain his popularity after admitting that his polio-stricken leg unmistakably displayed his own lack of faith.) The only remaining solution, for those who maintain that healing is ours, is to assert that in many cases healing will not be manifested until some indefinite, future time.

Claim It and Wait

Unfortunately, while granting that healing can be gradual, the faith teachers (along with many modern charismatic evangelists) continue to see their work as a replica of Jesus' own healing ministry. This conception sends them scurrying in search of gradual healings performed by Jesus. But there are none in the Bible.[23] It also opens them up to charges that their methods of healing are indeed different from those of Jesus: Jesus healed some diseases that today's healers tend to avoid; Jesus' healings were instantaneous, but most of today's are not; Jesus healed in response to specific requests or touched those whom he happened to meet, but many of today's healers set up large meetings and promise healing in advance; Jesus tended to avoid crowds, but many of today's healers seek them.[24]

These differences, though, do not necessarily invalidate forms of healing ministry found today. Both faith teachers and their critics have suffered from failing to distinguish clearly between gifts of miraculous healing (as done by Jesus, and as mentioned by Paul in 1 Corinthians 12) and the less spectacular ministry of healing that, according to the New Testament, seems to be the privilege of the church at large.[25] The letter of James, in the New Testament's most explicit teaching on prayer for healing, expresses a solid belief in God's healing power while giving no hint that recovery must be instantaneous: "Is any one of you sick? He should call the elders of the church to pray over him and anoint him with oil in the name of the Lord. And the prayer offered in faith will make the sick person well; the Lord will raise him up" (Jas 5:14-15). Similarly, Paul recognized God's hand in the healing of Epaphroditus, even though he suffered and nearly died before he regained his health.

Interpretation of this passage in James has not been unanimous. One commentator suggests that James intentionally used ambiguous words to include the possibility that the sick person might be spiritually if not physically healed.[26] But most have seen this as a wide-ranging promise establishing physical health as the norm for believers. The verb "raise up" implies that James has literal, bodily recovery in mind, and he speaks as if this "must have been normally the case."[27]

There seems to be a place, then, for healing through the prayer of faith—even if we are skeptical of (as I often am) the widely publicized, controversial twentieth-century phenomenon of mass healing rallies. Though their language at times is extreme, faith teachers, by affirming gradual healing and by approving doctors, become in practice little different from other Christians who recognize the already/not yet distinction and who take a more moderate view of healing. In short, when these balancing factors are included, we see that the faith message instructs sick people to pray with confidence, believe for the best and keep the doctor's phone number in the address book. Few Christians can object to that combination.

There remains one key difference: because they imply that Christians ought always to be healthy, faith teachers insinuate that the sick are to blame for their illness, even if there is no identifiable reason to hold them responsible for their suffering. This is a serious concern, since to imply to bewildered victims that their diseases are the product of their own failings can be devastating. At the same time, it becomes difficult to exercise strong faith in God's healing power if one begins to attribute failures to causes beyond our control. The path between these two dangers—undermining faith on the one hand and producing guilt on the other—is an extremely narrow one. But, as I will attempt to show (in chapter 10), I am convinced that it can be followed.

SIX

Does God Want You Wealthy?

T HE ONLY ONE WHO COULD POSSIBLY BELIEVE THIS nonbiblical nonsense is someone who wants to."[1]

This is one critic's response to the most brazen forms of prosperity preaching, which appeal to their hearers' desires for material comforts more often than they demand submission and obedience to God.

I sympathize with this critic's concern. I also have seen the distorted, selfish, "give-me" version of Christianity that the gospel of wealth can produce. And I agree that some leaders in the faith movement have made statements that can be—and have been—interpreted in just this way. But the faith teachings on prosperity do have redeeming features, though we will see that this is a point where the movement's harshest critics and wisest supporters are unable to agree even on what is being taught, let alone whether it is correct.

Critics of the movement have raised valid concerns—but so have the faith teachers. In an attempt to bring clarity and balance to the discussion I will first discuss areas where these teachers seem to go astray, then aspects of their work that appear to be valid and useful correctives.

Hundredfold Returns

When preaching their message of prosperity the faith teachers frequently quote Mark 10:29-30, where Jesus says, "I tell you the truth, . . . no one who has left home or brothers or sisters or mother or father or children or fields for me and the gospel will fail to receive a hundred times as much in this present age (homes, brothers, sisters, mothers, children and fields—and with them, persecutions) and in the age to come, eternal life." Gloria Copeland takes this promise very literally, at least as far as the possessions are concerned. She says that it gives us, if we have enough faith to receive it, the right to believe for a return of one thousand dollars on a ten-dollar contribution. She also stresses the words "in this present age," assuring us that this hundredfold return is an earthly, not just a heavenly reward. Jesus, she says, "did not say it would come in two weeks, but He said it would come in this life. . . . If we would exercise our faith, before we leave this life *all* that return would come to us" (emphasis hers).[2]

Her husband, Kenneth, is just as sweeping in his application of this passage, returning to it several times in his book *The Laws of Prosperity*. "Do you want a hundredfold return on your money?" he asks. "Give and let God multiply it back to you." In encouraging his readers to give financial support to teaching ministries, he writes, "Invest heavily in God; the returns are staggering, 100 to 1!" And again, "Every man who invests in the Gospel has a right to expect the staggering return of one hundredfold."[3]

But there are obvious problems with this interpretation. First, the faith teachers ignore the fact that Jesus included brothers, sisters, mothers and children, not just material belongings, as items to be reimbursed one hundredfold. Since no one is likely to literally receive a hundred mothers or two hundred children, we have here a clear hint that Jesus intended his words to be interpreted figuratively. Second, Jesus states that this promise is for those who have left everything to follow him; few of the faith teachers or their followers meet this qualification.[4] Third, these verses immediately follow a passage that reveals the spiritual danger, not the spiritual benefit, of riches. All these facts suggest that the interpretation of the hundredfold return promoted by the Copelands is incorrect.

The Blessings of Abraham

Their teaching on "Abraham's blessing," which they claim grants us liberty from both poverty and sickness, is equally controversial. The faith teachers base this doctrine on a comparison of one New Testament passage from Galatians 3 with one or two Old Testament quotations. Several of them point out that the promise God originally gave to the patriarch Abraham, recorded in Genesis 17, included the blessing of prosperity. They connect this passage with Paul's words in Galatians:

> Christ redeemed us from the curse of the law by becoming a curse for us, for it is written: "Cursed is everyone who is hung on a tree." He redeemed us in order that the blessing given to Abraham might come to the Gentiles through Christ Jesus. . . . If you belong to Christ, then you are Abraham's seed, and heirs according to the promise. (Gal 3:13-14, 29)

Since we are Abraham's seed, they conclude, the promise of prosperity is for us too. "Abraham's blessing is ours. . . . The first thing God promised Abraham was that He was going to make him rich."[5]

On other occasions Galatians 3 is connected with Deuteronomy 28, in which Moses promises blessings to the Israelites if

they obey the laws God gave them and threatens curses if they
fail to obey. Among the curses listed are poverty and sickness.
Seeing these curses as related to the law, followers of the faith
message often say that "Christ has redeemed us from the curse
of the law" (Gal 3:13) and therefore from both poverty and
sickness.[6]

Again, however, many have found fault with their explanations, objecting that the subject of Paul's discourse has nothing
to do with either of these Old Testament passages. A look at
the context of Galatians 3 suggests that the blessing to which
Paul refers is not freedom from poverty or sickness, but the
opportunity to be saved through faith and to receive the Holy
Spirit (see verses 8-9, 14). Whereas Deuteronomy 28 spoke of
the danger of violating the law of Moses, Galatians 3 teaches
that we no longer need to follow the law. In fact, for Paul the
law itself is the curse. Thus, the multiple curses of Moses and
the single curse of Paul seem totally unrelated to each other.
The only part of Abraham's blessing with which Paul is concerned is the promise that Gentiles along with Jews would one
day be included in God's people. Since Paul says nothing about
health or prosperity, it is a frail argument to promise these
benefits on the basis of this passage.[7]

"That Thou Mayest Prosper"

Even the "Old Faithful" of prosperity proof texts, 3 John 2, has
been the center of much dispute. Ever since Oral Roberts interpreted this passage in this way in the 1950s, charismatic
evangelists have quoted the apostle John's words, as translated
in the King James Version, as a demonstration of God's desire
that we may "prosper and be in health." The Copelands use
these words so often that they appear to be the key verse of
their ministry.[8] Yet Christians with stronger backgrounds in biblical study have repeatedly questioned the faith movement's
understanding of the verse.[9]

Read in context, 3 John 2 seems to be a personal wish for Gaius, the recipient of John's letter, not a divine promise for all Christians. Pentecostal scholar Gordon Fee has discovered that this verse is "the *standard* form of greeting in a personal letter in antiquity." He concludes, "To extend John's wish for Gaius to refer to financial and material prosperity for all Christians of all times is *totally foreign* to the text" (emphasis his).[10] Even without this background knowledge, readers of 3 John, if unfamiliar with the faith movement's use of verse 2, would be unlikely to find a timeless guarantee of financial blessing here. All the more so if they were reading a modern translation that replaces the verb phrase "that thou mayest prosper" with "that all may go well with you" as do the New International and Revised Standard Versions.

At best, it would seem, 3 John 2 places prosperity in the same category as sinlessness; both are qualities that God and God's people naturally desire but which, in this fallen world, do not always come to pass. The reason faith teachers tend to exaggerate the significance of John's wish and try very hard to find financial promises in places like Mark 10 and Galatians 3 is probably that the New Testament has very little good to say about material prosperity. Abundance of wealth is related to obedience frequently in the Old Testament but never by Jesus.[11]

This series of questionable interpretations causes some faith teachers—Kenneth Copeland among others—to make finance a more important part of Christianity than it really is. In one place, just a few sentences after he has wisely called money "only a very small part of prosperity," he calls finance "the biggest problem area on earth." If finance is truly our biggest problem, one would have expected Jesus and Paul to give it much more attention. But Copeland goes on to offer promises on slender biblical evidence, suggesting that those who know "God's system of finance . . . can absolutely believe God for anything in the world and get it!" With equal boldness Jerry Savelle teaches his readers to tell themselves, "If I am not prospering, . . . it is not God's fault, nor the fault of the Word of God—*it is my fault*" (emphasis added).[12]

The issue of prosperity, though, is one where not all the faith teachers can be held equally responsible. Copeland feels a special anointing to teach on this topic,[13] but Hagin definitely does not. Hagin's son pointed out in 1985 that not one of the roughly one hundred books and booklets the Hagins had produced centered primarily on prosperity. They see prosperity, he said, as "part of the package" available to Christians, but not as a main focus of the gospel.[14] The elder Hagin is said to have expressed doubts about literal interpretations of the hundred-fold return, because he has so seldom seen it come to pass.[15]

Sowing and Reaping Generously

Even those who unashamedly preach prosperity do not always need to reinterpret the Bible in defending their point. Anyone who cares to dispute that God's will is prosperity will have a difficult time explaining 2 Corinthians 9:6 where Paul promises his readers that "whosoever sows generously will also reap generously." If the Corinthians give the contributions Paul is requesting for the support of needy Christians, he says, they "will be made rich in every way."

The meaning of the word *rich* in this passage cannot be spiritualized, for the context is unquestionably one of finances, as Paul describes the material needs of Christians in other cities. Moreover, by explicitly linking generous giving with financial blessing, Paul shows that this connection is biblically sound and not just a shrewd ploy concocted by modern evangelists with expensive itineraries and multimedia ministries. As respected a teacher as nineteenth-century theologian Charles Hodge commented on this passage: "Giving is, to the natural eye, the way to lessen our store, not to increase it. The Bible says it is the way to increase it."[16]

In rightly interpreting Paul's message we must recall three balancing factors. First, he is communicating the promise of prosperity to a close-knit congregation, not telling each individual that he can count on being independently wealthy. Also, there is no sign that he made similar offers to the not-so-prosperous Christians destined to be the recipients of the Corinthians' generosity. Furthermore, Paul makes clear that these promised blessings are not primarily for our own benefit, but "so that you can be generous on every occasion."[17]

The prosperity preachers may have overlooked the first two of these factors, but on the last one—the importance of generosity—they deserve high marks. The Copelands and Savelle stress no aspect of their teaching more consistently than giving, and their dependability and insight in this area are worthy of commendation, even if the returns that they teach us to expect are sometimes inflated.

Gloria Copeland, for example, quotes 2 Corinthians 9 with a selflessness that no one can fault: "Don't just believe God to meet your needs. Believe Him for a surplus of prosperity so that you can help others. We here in America are a blessed people financially. We have been called to finance the gospel to the world." Kenneth Copeland agrees, stating that tithing (that is, giving ten per cent of our income) is the very least we should give before we can expect to receive, and that the mature Christian will not give with personal advantage primarily in mind. "The first step is to get your mind off of yourself," he teaches. "Begin to take up the needs of the body of Christ as if they were your own. . . . When you make it your purpose to feed the Gospel to the unsaved, God will support what you do. That is true prosperity!"[18]

Still more impressively, Jerry Savelle has devoted a complete book to the importance of giving. He makes extensive use of 1 Timothy 6:9-19, where Paul warns that "the love of money is a root of all kinds of evil" and commands the wealthy "to be rich in good deeds, and to be generous and willing to share." Savelle, whose deep concern for evangelism is apparent, insists that the main reason God wants his people to have money is so that they can reach millions with the gospel. "Do you know why God wants you rich? So you can do more," he states. "The wealthier you become, the more responsible you are to God."[19]

When Christians express this attitude and mean it, we can hope that they will be abundantly blessed. Richard Lovelace, an influential writer and catalyst in many Christian renewal activities, has been impressed, despite his concerns about the faith message, by those faith people who do seek to give, not to have. "The health-and-wealth emphasis," he writes, "makes sense when it is approached within a kingdom framework. . . . Believing that God can provide healing or funds essential for work in Christ's kingdom is a vital expression of faith."[20]

Redressing the Balance

The Copelands and Savelle seem to have at least the beginnings of this "kingdom framework." Unfortunately, many of their admirers do not; these people want to hear keys to financial blessings, not messages about putting God's kingdom ahead of their fleshly desires. Faith teachers are well aware of this problem, however, and on occasion they speak directly to those self-oriented listeners—though many who attack the faith teachers for propagating a man-centered theology have failed to take notice.[21] Gloria Copeland, for instance, rebukes the truncated religion practiced by people who want to receive from God but who are not willing to commit their lives to him. "If your motive is to be prosperous without serving God," she declares, "you had better read some other book. God's prosperity will work only in the life of the believer who is committed to the Word because he loves God."[22]

Kenneth Hagin, Jr., has sensed a need to deal with the same

imbalance. While asserting that God does provide prosperity for Christians, he is disgusted with students at his Rhema Bible Training Center "who talk about houses and Cadillacs." "The church doesn't exist for Christian prosperity," he sternly addressed one gathering of students. "If you came to this school with the idea that it is going to help you get more faith so you can have Cadillacs, I want you to resign today." He has continued to declare that Christians should be more concerned for the needy than for themselves, and that the church's prayers tend to be far too selfish.[23]

Jerry Savelle regrets these abuses too, for he feels that they cause the whole faith movement to be criticized for errors that he does not teach. In five separate passages in one of his books he complains about those who have distorted the truth of divine prosperity and mixed up their priorities and who "think that the faith message is a get-rich-quick message." Pained over the damage and strife that such people have caused—and over the fact that he and his fellow teachers are being blamed for it—he finally bursts out, "How I wish my critics would read this book!"[24]

Recently the Copeland ministry has taken a further step toward proper balance by emphasizing the relative nature of financial prosperity. In doing so it has responded to one of the most common criticisms of prosperity teaching, the objection that it must not be true because it cannot be applied all over the world. Several critics have lodged this objection, sometimes with unusually forceful disgust:

Let those who teach that all the redeemed ought to . . . have wealth go to Bangladesh and Cambodia with their teaching on prosperity. Let them preach their Wall Street gospel to the poverty-stricken masses and tell them to claim material goods. Any gospel that does not work equally well in the Congo or in Chicago is not the New Testament gospel.[25]

The gospel of prosperity must be limited to a few countries

of western Europe and the United States. Can you imagine
the absurdity of preaching to the underground church in
Russia that if they would only elevate the sights of their faith,
they could all be driving Cadillacs? . . . Thus faith theology
is bad theology; it is not universally applicable.[26]

What the critics hear convinces them that the faith teachers
could not work in the Third World. But it so happens that many
of them *have* worked in the Third World. The Copeland evangelistic team has ministered in the Philippines, unhesitantly
entering that country's poorer areas.[27] Hagin's magazine documents the work of his understudies and Bible-school graduates all over Central America and Africa. T. L. Osborn has
spent most of his career in Africa and, if his own materials can
be believed, has had greater success there than any other evangelist in this century.

In 1985 Kenneth Copeland finally incorporated his Third
World experiences into his writings. "Prosperity is relative," he
now states, and it is not primarily money. And he has visibly
publicized his support for Christian outreach in east Africa,
describing prosperity in such ordinary forms as plenty of rain
and plenty to eat.[28]

This movement toward a balanced perspective is encouraging, particularly since some of the faith teachers have expressed
their understanding of prosperity in a way that can "obscure
the gospel by sheer weight of attention."[29] It is true that the
Copelands define prosperity as "the ability to use God's ability
and power to meet the needs of mankind,"[30] and that in some
places they deal with spiritual and mental prosperity before the
physical blessings of health and wealth. But they refer so frequently to financial concerns and examples in their literature
that the word *prosperity,* when they use it, inevitably leads most
readers to think of finances.[31]

Copeland and others seem to have underestimated just how
effectively their gospel of wealth would tempt and incite human

lusts. But the pendulum may have reached its extreme and may be swinging back toward center. Nevertheless, there are biblical themes which the faith teachers still need to emphasize.

Jesus and Riches

Jesus had more to say about the abuse of wealth than about the dangers of poverty. In Luke 16, for example, he tells a parable in which the hero, a poor beggar named Lazarus, suffers hunger and sickness at the gate of a rich man who pays him no attention. The rich man dies and goes to hell, while Lazarus is taken to Abraham's bosom. If all believers were meant to prosper financially, it would seem that Jesus would not have wanted to confuse the issue by speaking approvingly of a man trapped at the very bottom of the economic ladder.

Jesus' story of the rich fool (Lk 12), enamored of his wealth but spiritually unprepared to face his eternal judgment, also illustrates how easily riches can become a snare rather than a blessing. The Lord makes the same point more bluntly in another sermon: "Do not store up for yourselves treasures on earth, where moth and rust destroy, and where thieves break in and steal. But store up for yourselves treasures in heaven" (Mt 6:19-20).

The lives of New Testament saints also seem to present a pattern in which prosperity does not always play a part. John the Baptist lived an ascetic life, dining on locusts and wild honey. Jesus told his disciples to take no extra belongings—not even a change of clothes—on their first missionary journey. Paul reports having experienced material lack during his ministry: "I know what it is to be in need" (Phil 4:12).

Perhaps no Scripture reflects this perspective on ministry more clearly than 1 Timothy 6:5. There Paul attacks "men of corrupt mind . . . who think that godliness is a means to financial gain." Despite the faith teachers' attempts to clarify their message, people are still receiving the impression that godliness guarantees gain. The message of 1 Timothy 6:5 is too seldom heard.[32]

The prosperity teachings also tend to spawn Christians who expect not only financial blessings, but lives of comfort and ease—a dangerous distortion of the Christian life. The faith movement should learn from Paul's second letter to the Corinthians. There we learn that the church at Corinth had a misconception of true spirituality, "looking only on the surface of things" (2 Cor 10:7) and preferring impressive-sounding "super-apostles" to Paul whose physical presence was less attractive. In response Paul boasts not of his triumphs but of his weaknesses: persecutions, dangers, hunger, sleeplessness and the thorn that kept him humble (2 Cor 11:23—12:10). Paul's insistence that these are the marks of a true apostle contradicts the notion that a successful Christian leader can be measured by wealth and popularity.

Jesus repeatedly emphasized that true Christian commitment would be costly. "If anyone would come after me," he said, "he must deny himself and take up his cross and follow me. For whoever wants to save his life will lose it, but whoever loses his life for me will find it" (Mt 16:24-25). As he warned one potential follower, "Foxes have holes and birds of the air have nests, but the Son of Man has no place to lay his head" (Mt 8:20). Faith teachers must place greater stress on these truths to balance their emphasis on the believer's authority and the blessings we can expect from God. These words of Jesus may not be comfortable, but Jesus never promised that the Christian life would be painless.

Faith teachers need to make a point of reminding listeners that some Christians may be called by God to a life of poverty in which only their most basic needs are met. Pillars of faith from Jeremiah to St. Francis of Assisi could not have fulfilled their callings without accepting material sacrifices. The same spirit is needed among Christians today, for believers living in first-rate suburban housing are seldom able to win the confidence of, and thus have a Christian impact on, the underprivileged who inhabit run-down inner-city areas.

The bottom line, it seems, is whether the faith teachers agree with Loren Cunningham's pithy statement: "God has promised to meet our needs, not our greeds."[33] Where the faith teachers are encouraging Christians to quit worrying about material concerns and trust God to "meet all [our] needs according to his glorious riches in Christ Jesus" (Phil 4:19), they are doing the body of Christ a great service. When they cause people to yearn for possessions they do not need, they are leading the body astray. Only the long-term commitment and stewardship of their followers will determine the impact of Copeland and his colleagues—whether it has been for good or for ill.

SEVEN

Name It and Claim It

W HEN A RETIRED FARMER—NO SCHOLAR OF GREEK—
takes it upon himself to tell scholars how to interpret a Greek
text, we suspect something has gone haywire. The farmer is
Charles Capps, one of the leading exponents of positive confession as it is being taught in America today. His writings are
proof that a good thing can be carried too far.

After twenty years of ineffective prayer, Capps decided to take
a fresh look at the Bible—and his life was never the same
again. Biblical prayer, he realized, requires confidence that
God will grant our requests, not the defeated uncertainty of
doubt. Capps began to exercise faith in God's promises, and he
found that God did not let him down.[1]

But as he began to write and speak about his discovery,
Capps encountered a problem that confronts every Bible teach-

er: he needed a consistent theology. He wanted to preach faith as the key to immediately answered prayer, but the Bible, complex book that it is, presented a few puzzles—and he would have to solve them.

One of those roadblocks was Luke 11:9, "Ask and it will be given to you." This verse posed a problem. Capps knew that the Amplified Bible (the version, a favorite among charismatics, that uses extra words to capture nuances of meaning) points out that the form of the Greek word "ask" implies a repeated action, better translated as "Ask and keep on asking." But Capps was convinced that this could not be right, for he had already read and digested the verses that guarantee answers to whatever we ask in faith. Besides, he had heard somewhere that in the lands where the Bible was written "The people understand, 'Ask once and you receive.' " So Capps felt safe in rejecting the Amplified Bible and a principle of Greek grammar.[2]

Capps had grasped a genuine principle of faith, but his excitement over that discovery had blinded him to other teachings that he perceived as contradictory. The form of the Greek verb used in Luke 11:9 does imply repeated action. Yet Capps boldly accused the Amplified Bible of giving readers "a false impression that will defeat them in their prayer life."[3]

Capps's inflexibility demonstrates a major flaw in positive confession teaching: it attempts to make universal laws out of isolated biblical texts. By encouraging Christians to believe that God intends them to live successful, victorious lives, the positive confession teachings are recovering an important, often forgotten part of the gospel. When they leave the sovereignty and guidance of the Holy Spirit out of the picture, however, they may be setting their followers up for failure and bitter discouragement.

Prayer that Works

Even if some of their teaching arouses concern, the positive-confession people merit recognition for taking seriously some biblical truths about faith and prayer that most Christians conveniently skip over. One of these often ignored passages, Mark 11:23-24, has become the keystone of Kenneth Hagin's ministry and of the positive confession movement in general:

> I tell you the truth, if anyone says to this mountain, "Go, throw yourself into the sea," and does not doubt in his heart but believes that what he says will happen, it will be done for him. Therefore I tell you, whatever you ask for in prayer, believe that you have received it, and it will be yours.

Even New Testament scholar Gordon Fee, no admirer of faith teachers, commends them for recovering this text from oblivion and rebelling against the typical style of prayer, in which people go through the motions but really don't expect anything to happen. As Fee so aptly puts it: "Even though evangelicals often pray, 'If it be Thy will, please heal so-and-so,' they would probably fall over in a dead faint if God actually answered their prayer."[4]

Faith teachers, in contrast, have no problem believing that the prayer of faith will change things. Rather, the charge lodged against the faith message is that it runs too far to the other extreme, stressing the power of our prayers so much that we become our own masters and the will of God is forgotten. Critics see this error exemplified in the following statement by Capps: "You have to believe that those things you say—everything you say—will come to pass. That will activate the God kind of faith within you, and those things which you say will come to pass." Hagin sounds much like Capps when he asserts that "it is unscriptural to pray, 'If it is the will of God.' When you put an 'if' in your prayer, you are praying in doubt."[5]

But the faith teachers are not as extreme as these quotations might suggest, for they know better than to take Mark 11:24 as a universal, unconditional promise. Hagin reminds his readers continually that they must confine their confessions to areas that are covered by biblical promises. "Do not get out beyond God's Word," he warns. He reports with dismay that most people who come to him for prayer, when he asks them, "What Scriptures are you standing on?" reply, "Well, not any in particular." He bluntly tells such people, "That's what you will get—nothing in particular."[6]

Fred Price has collected some colorful, though disturbing, anecdotes to show that Mark 11:24 has limitations. He has heard some people say, "I believe that I can eat as much of this cherry pie as I want and it is not going to make me fat." Then, when they gain weight, they wonder why Mark 11:24 didn't work for them! One woman in his church, Price relates, declared to the man of her dreams, "I claim you as my husband. You are going to be my husband, and there ain't nothing you can do about it." Price labels such cases exactly what they are— foolishness.[7]

The faith teachers must be given credit for their warnings that God will not answer requests that contradict the Bible or arise from wrong motives. But they do not seem to realize how these warnings affect their doctrine of positive confession. Clearly Jesus was using hyperbole in Mark 11—he wanted to encourage us to have faith, not to run around claiming absolutely whatever we want as ours. Yet the popular faith slogan, "You can have what you say," seems to imply just that. This emphasis becomes even more questionable when we recall (as we have seen in chapters five and six) that some of the promises offered by faith preachers have obscured large portions of Scripture. Although God's normal will for his people may be health and prosperity, some biblical heroes were sick, some were financially poor, some were rejected and some died as martyrs.

Larry Bishop of the Jesus People community in Chicago has made this point most clearly:

Once it is established that God will refuse *some* requests, then the whole idea of faith as a "force," operating unalterably in accordance with a formula, can no longer be sustained. Further, once we have affirmed that requests must be evaluated, in some way, then we have put it back into the hands of God to evaluate *all* requests (emphasis his).[8]

Write Your Ticket with God

While the faith teachers sometimes show proper respect for God's will, in other materials, such as Hagin's popular sermon "How to Write Your Own Ticket with God," that overriding consideration is barely noticeable. Hagin says that the four simple steps he received from the Lord—say it, do it, receive it, and tell it—will enable "anybody, anywhere" to "always receive what he wants" from God. Hagin's phrase "anything that the Bible promises you now," implies to the careful reader that we cannot get literally *anything* through these steps. And his illustrations—cases of physical healing and David's defeat of Goliath—do not embody blatant selfishness. Yet, even if unintentional, Hagin's message is capable of causing readers to treat God as giver only and not as Lord of their lives.[9]

Nevertheless, positive confession does have valuable uses. Capps, for example, encourages Christians to learn key Scriptures and recite them regularly in order to remind themselves that God wants to meet their needs, comfort and strengthen them, and free them from the bondage of worry and fear.[10] Though some of the verses he selects seem to have been taken out of context, the general idea that God's Word can conquer negativism and bring victory is a true and proper emphasis.

Similarly, most would agree that there is a connection between positive thinking and physical and mental health. As the book of Proverbs counsels, "A cheerful heart is good medicine" (17:22).

The most important contribution the world view of positive confession has to offer probably concerns the relationship between prayer and God's will. This is a hotly disputed topic, but

the faith teachers have plenty of New Testament Scriptures to
show that those who seek diligently after God can often find
God's will for their lives and then pray for it without wavering.
Most Christians seem to pray with little confidence, committing
themselves to whatever the Lord desires for them but seldom
knowing just what he does desire. In contrast, the faith teachers
are serious about teaching people to earnestly seek and consistently receive divine guidance.[11]

"If you remain in me and my words remain in you," said
Jesus, "ask whatever you wish, and it will be given you" (Jn
15:7). "Ask and you will receive, and your joy will be complete"
(Jn 16:24). Jesus clearly presupposes that we mortals can know
God's will well enough to pray confidently, and there is nothing
in the text to suggest that this privilege was intended only for
the early church.

This truth is strengthened in two striking passages in 1 John
that bear little resemblance to our generally mundane prayer
lives. "If our hearts do not condemn us," John firmly asserts,
"we have confidence before God and receive from him anything we ask" (1 Jn 3:21-22). "If we ask anything according to
his will, he hears us. And if we know that he hears us—whatever we ask—we know that we have what we asked of him"
(1 Jn 5:14-15). Here too, of course, there are clear conditions of
obedience and conformity to the divine will. Nevertheless, once
the conditions are met, the promises are surprisingly broad.

Paul Yonggi Cho, Korean pastor of the world's largest church
and to some extent a partaker of positive confession theology,
offers help putting these Scriptures into practice in an unselfish
way. His book *The Fourth Dimension,* while containing some
questionable passages,[12] invites us to seek God's will in order
that our praying might be more effective.

Cho recommends putting ourselves "in neutral gear," waiting
on the Lord, willing to accept whatever direction God should
choose. "I don't wish to make decisions for my own benefit,"

he tells God, "but to decide according to Your desire." It is only after taking this step that we can expect to receive specific guidance from God and act with assurance of success. "The Lord wants to cleanse your life and make you surrendered to him," Cho cautions. "The Lord will never give promises promiscuously."[13]

Lord Willing

As with prosperity, the key is willingness to follow God wherever he leads. This is the prerequisite to receiving blessings and answered prayers. Faith teachers, though they sometimes make this connection, in other places seem determined to destroy the link between submission to God and receiving his blessings. Hagin, for instance, takes great pains to distinguish prayers of consecration (that is, personal devotion or commitment) from the "prayer to receive from God." He says that, when Jesus prayed to God "if you are willing" in the garden of Gethsemane, this was a prayer of consecration, not a prayer of petition. When we are dedicating our lives to God, Hagin feels it is acceptable to ask God what his will is. But "when it comes to changing things or getting something from God . . . we know it is His will that our needs be met." " 'If' . . . should not be in your prayers when you are trying to change a situation."[14]

The problem with Hagin's view is that petition and consecration cannot be so easily separated. No one was more intent on "trying to change a situation" than Jesus in Gethsemane when he prayed, "Father, if you are willing, take this cup from me." Similarly, despite some teachers' efforts to insist otherwise,[15] it appears that Jesus is fully satisfied by faith like that of the leper who came to him begging, *"If you are willing,* you can make me clean" (Mk 1:40, my emphasis).

In short, though their desire to encourage strong faith is biblical, the faith teachers miss the mark when they try to establish inviolable laws by which faith is supposed to operate.

They are absolutely correct when they tell us that our faith in the Word of God should be as instinctively trusting as our faith in the laws of electricity, and at least as confident as our faith that our boss will pay us at the end of the week. As the Bible teaches, there are times when we should pray with boldness. But to remove the "if" from all our petitions ignores passages like James's assertion that those who think they know precisely God's plan for their future are actually guilty of false boasting. "You do not even know what will happen tomorrow," James reproaches such people. "Instead, you ought to say, 'If it is the Lord's will, we will live and do this or that' " (Jas 4:15-16).[16]

The familiar story of the three men in the fiery furnace, yet another case of "if" praying, has evoked some fascinating interpretation from the faith movement. Shadrach, Meshach and Abednego, even while courageously sharing their faith with the king, appear to admit that God may let them die in the furnace: "The God we serve is able to save us from it, and he will rescue us from your hand, O king. But even if he does not, we want you to know, O king, that we will not serve your gods or worship the image of gold you have set up" (Dan 3:17-18). Critics of the faith message point out that the men, rather than holding to a positive confession, expressed uncertainty about the outcome of their torture and were not chastised by God for doing so.[17]

Gloria Copeland, ironically, cites this same passage as an example of a "right mental attitude." In quoting it, she deletes the crucial words "But even if he does not" from verse 18, although she does indicate that part of the verse has been omitted. Without support from the passage, she asserts that the three men "went into the fire fully intending to come out."[18]

The Power of Negative Confession

Hagin, Jr., has dealt with this story less evasively. He states that the three Israelites "had such a commitment that they were willing to make what some people call a negative confession."[19]

He does not make clear whether he himself considers it a negative confession, or how this story can be reconciled with the Hagins' standard teaching in this area. But at least he does not avoid a passage that does not mesh well with his theology.

The elder Hagin also has made statements that, if applied consistently, could moderate the extremes of positive confession. In discussing physical healing, for example, he generously states that God is willing to accept whatever faith we have. "God does not leave us stranded," he says. "If we cannot rise to meet Him on His level, He will come down to meet us on ours."[20]

So far, so good. But then Hagin seems to nullify his wisdom as he explains the distinction between faith and hope. This is his description of what often occurs after he prays confidently with a sick person:

I open my eyes and say, "Brother (or Sister), is it done?"

Eight times out of ten they start bawling, "Brother Hagin, I sure *hope* it is."

I have to tell them. "It isn't. It isn't. I'm *believing* and you're *hoping*. There is no agreement here. It didn't work."[21]

Whereas Jesus was willing to heal a boy whose father confessed, "I do believe; help me overcome my unbelief" (Mk 9:24), Hagin tells us that sick people must declare themselves healed immediately at the conclusion of prayer if they are to expect a positive answer.

Other faith teachers have taken their positive confessions far outside the realm of reality. Capps is the undisputed leader here, lifting biblical teaching on the power of the tongue out of its context. When the apostle James tells us that the tongue "defileth the whole body, and setteth on fire the course of nature" (3:6 KJV), the context is clearly one of evil, unwholesome talk and its spiritual effects. Capps reads the passage in terms of physical health, however, and tells us that we should not speak of sickness lest we bring sickness on ourselves. "The tongue can destroy the very course of nature that causes you to be healthy," he says. "If you begin to say, 'I believe I'm coming down with something,' you probably will."[22]

It is statements like these that leave critics wondering how the faith message differs in substance from the irrationality of Christian Science, which teaches us simply to deny the existence of sin, sickness and death. In general, it is unfair to equate faith teaching with Christian Science, since faith teaching shows much more respect for biblical authority and the person of Jesus than do the ingenious but indefensible interpretations of Christian Science founder Mary Baker Eddy.[23] But Capps's teachings seem to partially justify these concerns. Fortunately, other pieces of faith literature have helped to restore order. Hagin, Jr., speaks directly to the issue: "When you're sick, you've got to recognize that you're sick. 'I'm not going to speak that into existence!' they [i.e., misguided believers] say. You don't have to. It's a fact. If you hurt, you hurt."[24]

The positive confession teachers also run into considerable dissent when they speak of "claiming," by faith, events or blessings that have not yet happened. The elder Hagin freely admits that this has been an especially controversial area but cites Romans 4:17 on his behalf, noting that in this passage God "calls things that are not as though they were."[25]

The logical, common objection to this argument is that the fact that God can do something does not mean that we can do it. Hagin has attempted to answer this objection, but most of his rebuttal suffers from the same flawed logic. "If it is wrong for me to call things which be not as though they were," he begins, "it is wrong for God to do it." Quoting Ephesians 5:1 ("Be imitators of God"), he adds, "Children of God ought to act like God." If Hagin's statements were universally true, though, then either we should be declaring ourselves Lord of the universe (since God has done so), or else it is wrong for God to make himself Lord (since we cannot do so).[26]

If Hagin's version of positive confession is problematic,

Capps's version is worse. We can only hope that Capps, like Jesus in Mark 11, intended to use hyperbole, or that his readers will not interpret his statements literally. Surely he did not actually mean to make God subservient to our words when he wrote, "Words are the most powerful thing in the universe."[27] But that is just one of his many spectacular sayings. Here are others:

"Faith will work without prayer."

"We have brought sickness and disease into our vocabulary, and even death. . . . When we say, 'That tickled me to death,' *that is contrary to the Word of God"* [emphasis his].

"We have said, 'Oh, it looks like the wicked prosper.' Well, we said they were. That is one reason they are prospering."

"You don't always obey what someone else says, but you do obey your words. They govern you."[28]

Hidden Dangers

Capps seems to have embraced a theological error that could have serious consequences if not curbed. He would have us believe that God cannot act in our lives unless we release God's ability through faith.

The angels . . . are busy to perform or cause to come to pass the things you speak if they are in agreement with the Word of God. By authority of your words, they will maneuver you into a position where these things will come to pass.

But if you speak sickness and disease, if you speak contrary to the Word of God, they will . . . back off, fold their hands, and bow their heads for you have bound them by the words of your mouth. Your words will either bind them or loose them. If your words bind the angels, you have bound God's messengers and, in so doing, you have bound God.[29]

According to Capps, then, God is waiting for us to initiate and pursue our relationship with him. This view clearly conflicts with the biblical view of salvation, for according to the Scriptures God is the initiator and we are the respondents. While we were yet sinners Christ died for us. It was God who reconciled the world to himself, not us; we did not invite Christ into the world. We are saved only through God's grace and mercy.[30] Of course, we must respond by accepting his grace and obeying his Word, yet this is all due to God's prior offer of redemption. And our overwhelming indebtedness to God does not change after we are saved. Rather, Paul says, we must not set aside the grace of God. Whatever gifts or abilities we have received come to us by grace, and throughout our lives we must return to that throne of grace to obtain God's help.[31]

We are not quibbling over a fine point of theology—how we relate to God makes a difference. Those who are conscious of their need for God's grace live with gratitude to God, recognize God as their sole provider and are willing to submit all their gifts to the Lord's direction. But those who think of themselves as primarily responsible for their own salvation and spiritual growth soon become either prideful (if successful) or guilt-ridden (if not). In either case, spiritual ruin results from this tendency to maximize human responsibility and forget God's undeserved grace.[32]

The notion that everything is subject to "spiritual laws" can lead to even more serious dangers. Those who teach this seem to imply that human beings, if they learn how to use spiritual laws, can control their world. Combined with the premise—occasionally suggested by some faith teachers—that "we are gods," it leads toward a mindset in which humble submission to God is irrelevant and unnecessary, since we have the power to obtain what we want by applying "spiritual law." If the faith message ever takes this form, it will be no more Christian than is a spiritualist who includes Bible verses in his séances and formulas.[33]

To curb this excess, faith teachers need to heed the message of Hebrews 11, which describes faith not as a tool to get blessings but as the means by which we obey God. The writer of Hebrews reminds us of those biblical heroes who were tortured, flogged, imprisoned or killed—and he concludes, "these were all commended *for their faith*" (Heb 11:39, my emphasis). We too must be willing to use our faith in such uncomfortable ways if God should so desire.

Many of the ideas underlying positive confession have genuine merit. But a variety of dangers is implicit in the form these teachings have taken within faith circles. If the faith movement is hoping to influence the rest of Christianity, it must weed out these problems that have caused many outsiders to totally reject the movement.[34]

Does the Bible Really Say That?

*T*AKE TWO CHRISTIANS COMMITTED TO THE AUTHORITY of the Bible. Close them up in a room with instructions to talk about their faith. In nine cases out of ten they will find more to agree on than to disagree over. Why, then, do the faith teachers seem to run into disagreements on practically every front? The storm surrounding the faith movement suggests that the differences involved are deeper than ordinary. In fact, the problem is that the faith movement and its critics, in practice if not in theory, do not agree on how to go about interpreting Scripture.

One of the first rules of interpretation is that any passage must be read in its original context, so that its author's intention may be understood. The faith teachers do not dispute this principle. Charles Capps states, "If you take Scripture out of context, you can make the Bible say anything you want it to say. . . . The last and greatest of all deceptions is to take the Word out of context and distort it to make it say something different from the true meaning." Kenneth Hagin, echoing Capps's stated concern for contextual interpretation, has written, "It is foolish to take a text out of its setting and try to prove something with it." His son concurs, noting, "I can create any doctrine I want by pulling Scriptures out of context."[1] So the battle is not over whether such a rule exists and is valid, but whether the faith preachers obey it. There is evidence that they do not.

They employ the same distortion of Proverbs 6:2, for example, that we have seen in the theology of Hobart Freeman. In context, the phrase "thou art snared with the words of thy mouth" (Prov 6:2 KJV) is part of a warning not to make unwise commitments in financial dealings. In the works of many faith teachers, however, this passage becomes a universal principle and is applied to everything we say.[2]

Another passage consistently put to unexpected use is Hebrews 3:1 (KJV): "Consider the Apostle and High Priest of our profession, Christ Jesus." Faith preachers point out that the Greek word for profession (translated "confession" in other versions) literally means "saying the same thing." Thus they have concluded from this verse that we must speak with our mouths the same things that God says about us (that is, positive confessions) in order to be blessed by God. But this application of the passage appears to be far removed from what the author of Hebrews had in mind.[3] The context of the verse shows that the "confession" described here is the readers' commitment to Christ, not any form of "positive confession." The writer is simply admonishing his readers to live up to the Christian commitment they are assumed to have made.

Of course the faith teachers are not always so flippant in their analysis of Scripture. But these examples and others not quite so flagrant have produced concern and confusion among

Christians. Equally suspect, to many observers, is an occasional tendency to interpret the Bible in a highly speculative manner, assuming facts that are not given in the Bible and cannot be proved.

The Perils of Speculation

An example of speculative interpretation is Capps's understanding of Peter's imprisonment in Acts 12. The passage tells us that, though the church was earnestly praying for Peter, they refused to believe Rhoda, the woman who answered his knock and announced he was at the door, so astonished were they at his miraculous release. This case presents difficulties for Capps, because the people's surprise implies that they were not praying with the assurance that Capps considers necessary for successful prayer. So Capps supplements the text with his own speculation.

> I really believe that Rhoda was the only one in that whole prayer group that had prayed in faith. . . . The way [the others] talked, I suspect that they were praying the problem. If it hadn't been for someone praying and believing the answer, they would have prayed Peter right into his grave.[4]

To base one's doctrine of prayer on such subjective musing, as Capps does, is a most unwise and dangerous procedure.

Kenneth Copeland, explaining why Jesus told a rich young man (in Mk 10:17-23) to give away all his possessions, engages in similar speculative interpretation, mixing it with words often used by many Christian teachers: "The Lord spoke to me." Jesus' stern command to this rich man seems to contradict Copeland's doctrine of financial prosperity. But Copeland thinks the true explanation of the passage has been revealed to him: When he was reading about this rich man's faithfulness in observing the Jewish law, he says, "The Lord spoke to me and said, 'See, this is why he was rich.' " Copeland goes on to imply that the man would have become even richer by giving to the Lord: "This was the biggest financial deal that young man had ever been offered, but he walked away from it because he didn't know God's system of finance."[5]

All this may sound comfortable, and ingenious, but it is pure speculation. There is nothing in the text to suggest that this man's wealth was linked to his obedience, or that the two should always go together. (Remember that Elijah and John the Baptist were very obedient but without wealth, and that tax collectors of Jesus' day were wealthy without obedience.) Nor is there any hint that Jesus wanted the man to view his giving as a "financial deal." Rather, Copeland seems to have superimposed his presuppositions on this text in such a way as to make it say what it does not. And his confidence that the Lord gave him this interpretation does not guarantee its truth. On the contrary, all sorts of non-Christian sects, from Mormonism to the Moonies, have been born out of a special revelation that someone claimed to have received directly from the Lord.[6]

Gloria Copeland deals in a similar way with Paul's inability to get rid of his "thorn in the flesh."

God had given Paul the revelation of the authority of the believer. Paul had authority over Satan in the name of Jesus just as you and I do; and to get results, he had to enforce his authority by directly commanding the evil spirit to desist in his maneuvers against him. Instead, Paul sought deliverance from the Lord. . . .

When Paul asked the Lord that this messenger of Satan depart from him, the Lord said, "My grace is sufficient for thee: for my strength is made perfect in weakness" (2 Cor. 12:9). He did not say that the messenger would not depart. He was saying to Paul, "My favor is enough. For when you do not have the ability to humanly overcome, *you* use *My* name to stop Satan's attacks and cast out the devil" (emphasis in original).[7]

How Copeland makes the leap from "My grace is sufficient for thee" to "use My name to stop Satan's attacks" is not at all clear. On the basis of this logic, though, she concludes that Paul prayed to God when he should have simply flexed his spiritual authority and ordered the evil spirit to leave. In other words, she dares to state, even though Paul admits to no lack, that he displays his ignorance of the principles of spiritual warfare. In response it must be asked: How do we know *from the text* that Paul was wrong? If we decide that Paul was wrong here, how can we be sure that he is trustworthy in other places?

Whereas unusual interpretations of God's Word sometimes result from speculation, at other times they appear to reflect lack of study. The clearest illustration of this problem I have seen comes from satellite pastor Bob Tilton. He has encouraged followers to write their prayer needs on a piece of paper, touch the page while praying for them, and then send the page to Tilton so that he can do the same. His basis for this practice is Matthew 18:19 (KJV): "If two of you shall agree on earth as touching anything that they shall ask, it shall be done for them of my Father which is in heaven." However, a glance at any modern translation shows that the word translated "touching" by King James's scholars actually means "concerning" (much as we might say, "It was a sermon touching on three main issues") and has nothing to do with where we place our fingers. Perhaps Tilton knows this and is only making a pun, but he gives the impression of lacking the basic knowledge needed to teach the Bible reliably.[8]

Revelation Knowledge

In addition to all these interpretive stumblings, the faith teachers have gotten into further trouble over the concept of "revelation knowledge." Critics have understood this concept to be, in effect, a denial of biblical authority and have connected it with the extremes illustrated by one Rhema Bible Training Center student who told an inquirer, "I don't have to read my

Bible devotionally anymore because I get [my guidance] direct."[9]

Actually, though, the major teachers utterly repudiate practices like this. In fact, Hagin has singled out for criticism an example very similar to that of the Rhema student.

A minister who at one time was very sound said, "I don't need that book any more. I am beyond that." Then he threw the Bible on the floor. "I have the Holy Ghost. I am a prophet. God sends my instructions direct." It was not long until he was prophesying that people should each give him a hundred dollars. He was getting his instructions direct—but directly from where?[10]

The theme of submitting prophecy to the Word of God is a consistent theme in Hagin's writings, and his concern for putting the Bible first is unmistakable.[11]

Normally, the faith teachers describe revelation knowledge as the result of direct, personal study of the Scriptures. Gloria Copeland speaks of letting the Bible's words "become a powerful reality in my spirit." She adds, "The Word is the seed. If it is planted in the heart and allowed to grow and increase, it will come to maturity and produce the harvest of results." Revelation knowledge came from prophets in Old Testament times, before most of the Bible was recorded, but today the place to look for it is in the Bible.[12]

Hagin, like Copeland, repeatedly directs his readers to the Bible as their source of "spiritual revelation."[13] However, one of his references to revelation knowledge serves only to add fuel to the controversy. Referring with admiration to E. W. Kenyon's *The Wonderful Name of Jesus*, from which he quotes copiously in his own book *The Name of Jesus*, Hagin declares: "It is revelation knowledge. It is the Word of God."[14] In capitalizing "Word," Hagin appears to be placing Kenyon's word on a par with the true Word of God—the Bible.

Jerry Savelle also seems to think of revelation knowledge as a modern, newly discovered interpretation of the Bible. Regarding a series of teachings he gave on divine prosperity, his ministry catalog reads, "The revelation knowledge in this set was given to Brother Savelle supernaturally by God. . . . All the seals have been taken off God's Word. There is an outpouring of revelation knowledge in our generation."[15]

Does this reflect a biblical desire (see 1 Cor 2:6-13) to receive knowledge from the Holy Spirit, or does it represent a trend toward making private revelations equally authoritative with the Bible? A difficult question. But if Paul was able to have the mind of Christ in the first century (1 Cor 2:16), I do not know why we should need to have seals removed from God's Word through special revelation to an evangelist in the twentieth century. In any case, the ways in which faith teachers quote personal revelations, prophecies or visions give added cause for concern. Hagin attributes one of his most controversial sermons directly to a vision of Jesus; he recreates a lengthy conversation with the Lord in which God taught him about prosperity. And, as we have noted, "The Lord told me" is often used by faith preachers as their source of authority.[16]

A Question of Authority

A look at the tests given by the Hagin ministry's correspondence course further reveals this trend. The tests consist almost exclusively of true-false questions, thus causing respondents to treat the faith teachers' revelations and interpretations as fact, not as opinion. Here is one of the most striking questions (to which the "correct" answer is *true*): "Jesus told Charles Capps, 'I have told my people they can have what they say, and they are saying what they have.' "[17] Though the faith teachers may justifiably say that they intend only to clarify the message of the Bible, their interpretation remains imperfect and fallible. To treat their words and revelations as if they were indisputably true (as the correspondence course seems to do) is extremely dangerous.

One charismatic pastor has told me a story illustrating that this true-false method of teaching encourages automatic acceptance and discourages questioning or independent thinking. The pastor's wife, during a women's Bible study, expressed disagreement with a positive-confession comment made by another participant. After pointing out what the Bible said on that topic, she was unsettled to hear the woman who had made the original statement reply, "But Kenneth Copeland says . . ."—as if Copeland's words held equal or even superior authority to Scripture. Copeland and other faith teachers, of course, would disavow this use of their messages. Hagin, I am told, explicitly instructs his students to reject anything he says if they find that it is not in line with the Bible. But in introducing new doctrines and interpretations of Scripture by "divine revelation," without calling on their followers to continually exercise their own discernment, they are treading a path that could lead to cultism, and they must be held partly responsible for the resulting abuses.

The cases where faith teachers supplement the Bible with speculation, interpret it in novel ways or begin to undermine biblical authority by emphasizing personal revelations have many Christians worried about where the movement is headed. Gordon Fee, one of the Pentecostal-charismatic movement's most widely respected Bible scholars, has carefully examined the faith teachers' approach to the Scriptures and has found it faulty in several ways. He is greatly distressed at "the purely subjective and arbitrary way [health and prosperity preachers] interpret the biblical text." He finds in the faith movement a tendency to misinterpret key scriptures, to choose their texts selectively while omitting others and thus to display "a failure to understand the essential theological framework of the New Testament writers."[18]

In this chapter I have given examples illustrating the errors in biblical interpretation that may be found within the faith movement. We have seen other examples in previous chapters. In view of these problems, many Christian friends and scholars have argued for the outright rejection of the faith movement and have considered my own degree of tolerance overly generous. They have good reasons for saying so, as these mishandlings of Scripture are a justifiable cause for concern. It is my opinion, however, that under the proper conditions faith teachings can have—and, in many cases, actually have had—a positive impact. As we turn to studying how these faith teachings have been implemented, we will see some of the conditions that can make them either horribly crippling or uniquely inspirational.

NINE

The Faith Teachings in Real Life

THE ADMIRERS OF HAGIN, COPELAND AND THEIR COL-
leagues purchase the books and pamphlets of their favorite
evangelists and are blessed with story upon story, recounting
stunning interventions of the supernatural into daily experience. Bank accounts swell. The deaf hear. The lame walk.
Heavenly visions abound. There is instruction and guidance
from Jesus, who introduces the heavenly visions, revealing
knowledge about other people that the evangelists could not
have known otherwise.

Perhaps the most unforgettable of these episodes is Hagin's
tour of hell.

I went down, down, down, until the lights of the earth faded
away. . . . The further down I went, the hotter it was and the
more stifling it became. . . . I sensed that one more foot, one

more step, one more yard, and I would be forever gone and could not come out of that horrible place. . . .

A voice spoke from far above the blackness, above the earth, and above the heavens. It was the voice of God. I did not see Him and I do not know what He said because He did not speak in English. He spoke some other tongue. When He spoke it reverberated throughout the region of the damned, shaking it like a leaf in the wind and causing that creature [who was escorting Hagin to hell] to relax his grip on my arm. I did not turn around, but there was an unseen power that pulled me, and I came away from the fire, away from the heat, back into the shadows of the absorbing darkness.

I began to ascend until I came to the top of the pit and saw the light of the earth. I came back into that room just as real as at any other time I had entered it through the door, with the exception that my spirit needed no doors. I slipped back into my body as a man slips into his trousers in the morning, the same way in which I had gone out—through my mouth.[1]

These admirers seldom stop with reading books. They listen to their favorites' tapes and radio programs and tune them in on television. Many of them make special plans and travel hundreds of miles to attend these preachers' revival campaigns and conventions. Some of them devote two years to full-time study at Hagin's Bible school, learning how to have a ministry with signs and wonders.

But when they return from these glorious experiences, many of them must face a painfully mundane reality. There is, predictably, dispute over just how many miracles are actually happening, but it appears that unmistakable supernatural interventions are less common in most places than is reported in Tulsa. Elsewhere, it often seems, the sick who come forward for prayer do not recover any more quickly than the doctors had predicted. Not many congregations are financially wealthy, and few individuals are reporting major upturns or surprising economic blessings. Sometimes there is little money available to pay the pastor. The congregation's numerical growth is slow.[2]

While some faith pastors seem to be vastly successful, many of them and their church members are forced to ask themselves, at some point, the inevitable question: Why are Hagin, Copeland and Tilton's miracles so numerous and ours so rare? Are we doing something wrong? Are we blocking the flow of God's power through sin or unbelief?

A Practical Dilemma for the Faithful

These admirers of the faith teachers face a painful dilemma. For doubting the honesty or reliability of the movement's leading figures is not an option. The dilemma has just two horns: either (1) there *is* something wrong with the local fellowship (or the individual), causing it (him/her) to function at a level far below what God desires, or (2) the comparative lack of miracles suggests simply that God works differently with different people, and there is no major cause for alarm.[3]

The nationally known teachers are not, by any means, the only people reporting success and miracles. But even in solid faith churches, divine health and prosperity are not universal. There remain some sick or struggling people in these congregations, forcing the disciples of faith teachings to deal with the dilemma and choose, instinctively if not consciously, between the two possible explanations. Which one they choose has immense bearing on the effects of their ministry and witness, both to other Christians and to a skeptical but curious world. By examining the consequences of both responses to the dilemma, and analyzing some of the dynamics of the faith movement, we can see how and why it has produced both bad and good fruit.

Joni Eareckson Tada has had plenty of experience with people who have committed themselves to the first horn of the dilemma: if miracles are not happening, something is wrong. Tada broke her neck in a 1967 diving accident and spent her late teen-age years fighting to put together a meaningful life as a quadriplegic and trying to understand why God would let such a disaster happen to her.[4] Spiritually she is wonderfully rehabilitated, as her three books and a movie about her life have graphically portrayed. Physically she is not. And this fact has destined her for encounters with those who think that real faith would heal her.

During the years after her injury she heard many times the arguments we have already examined in chapters four and five. Christians encouraged her to seek healing. By 1972 she was convinced that they were right. She brought together a group of friends and church leaders and set up a private healing service. The week before that service, she publicly confessed her faith by telling people, "Watch for me standing on your doorstep soon; I'm going to be healed." On the scheduled day the group read Scriptures, anointed her with oil and prayed in fervent faith. Today, fifteen years later, she is still a quadriplegic. Her case remains a potential embarrassment to those who are committed to the first horn of our dilemma. For Tada did everything right and seemed to have met all the conditions, yet she was not healed.[5]

With Christians across the United States echoing the teaching that faith is the only missing ingredient needed to produce healing, many thousands have heard the same counsel that Tada received. At a charismatic church near my home, one of the elders, who is confined to a wheelchair, reports that people often express surprise that he is still handicapped. Debby Zook has recorded similar experiences with well-intentioned advice and the frustration it brings. Debby is blind. She has deflected criticisms of the level of her faith by noting that "I receive answers to my other prayers." In a friend's life she has spotted one pitfall in the constant quest for healing: "It was obvious to me that she was focusing her entire life and all her energies toward this goal. In all of her efforts, she was clearly miserable and missing out on life."[6] While they spend their energy trying to find healing, the sick miss God's other plans and opportunities.

In the face of such cases as Tada and Zook, outsiders often wonder how anyone can continue to hold that all who come to God with real faith will be made whole. What these outsiders fail to realize is that it is impossible to disprove this view. Faith is not a measureable quantity; there exists no "faith meter" which we can attach to Tada to determine whether she had attained the minimum level of faith required to make her limbs functional again. Because it depends on unverifiable premises regarding what faith is and how it works, this aspect of the faith message is difficult to refute. Its adherents can always take safe, if questionable, refuge in the argument that something (though nobody knows just what) was deficient in Tada when she and her friends prayed, or that Zook has more faith in her other prayers than in her requests for healing. The rest of us can call them wrong, if we wish, but we have no grounds for calling them irrational.[7]

Nevertheless, those who take this inflexible stance—that only human error of some sort can prevent healing from occurring—put considerable pressure on themselves. Unlike Kathryn Kuhlman, who attributed the whole process to the Holy Spirit, and Oral Roberts, who has freely admitted that many for whom he prays go away unimproved, these teachers have left no room for failure. When failure does occur, they have no choice but to cruelly heap insult upon injury by telling the sick person that he or she must have some spiritual problem.

Some Sad and Strange Stories
A theology of guaranteed healing sometimes results in ministry techniques that strike uninvolved observers as strange if not

ludicrous. My most memorable observation of such behavior occurred at a revival meeting conducted by a traveling evangelist on a midwestern university campus. After completing his rousing message, this evangelist entered the healing portion of his ministry. As is often the case in charismatic services, several of the apparent healings involved lengthening of a leg that had previously been too short to match its partner. Near the end of the service a paralyzed student rolled himself forward in his wheelchair. The evangelist apparently had already met the student, for he called the young man by name, stated that God could heal him completely some day and proceeded to pray for the lengthening of one of his legs. After about a minute of agonizing, the speaker and the local leader announced that they had succeeded. But this was a rather useless miracle (if it was a miracle at all) since the man's legs, though perhaps now of equal length, were still paralyzed. There was no indication that the paralyzed man lacked faith for total healing. He was not even asked how much faith he had. I was left wondering if it was the evangelist himself who lacked the faith to pray for a healing that could be verified.

In another city a pastor arose sheepishly to instruct his congregation on a ticklish concern. Some of the church members, he had heard, were spreading contagious diseases among the church's little ones by bringing their sick babies to the nursery. Against the nursery volunteers' protests, these parents were positively confessing that their children were well. Since the parents had claimed their healing, there was nothing to worry about. They may have been dismissing those persistent whines and coughs as lying symptoms, but those lying symptoms proved to be contagious, and only an announcement from the pulpit could succeed in putting an end to the problem.

I wish that all the stories were as humorous and inconsequential as this nursery tale. But they are not. No phenomenon of "hyper-faith" (that is, abuses of faith teaching) has been so destructive as the ungracious treatment of the sick and dying. I have been appalled to hear countless stories of well-meaning believers, their sense of compassion overshadowed by their theology, shattering the composure of seriously ill friends by telling them that they lack faith. Forgetting that faith works by love, they destroy faith and cause outsiders to mock the charismatic movement and reject the gospel of Christ. The faith teachers can only enhance the integrity of their ministries and message by denouncing unkindness done in the name of Christ.[8]

Those who get carried away with the gospel of healing can bring not just emotional but physical pain on themselves and others. Jimmy Swaggart, one of the faith message's loudest critics, recalls the night when he received a phone call from a woman he knew. Her husband had repeatedly blacked out while driving on their vacation. Against Swaggart's pleas they followed the guidance of another preacher who "advised that they not deny his healing by consulting a doctor." A few weeks later the man blacked out again while driving and crashed into another car. Fortunately, no one was seriously hurt. This time he agreed to visit a physician, who found an abnormality in his blood pressure that was easily remedied.[9] One can hardly blame Swaggart, after he has personally shared in this unnecessary near-disaster, if his anger toward the faith movement as a whole sometimes seems unrestrained.

"If they were going to claim this healing," Swaggart says of this man and his wife, "it seemed logical to them to proclaim their faith by refusing to consult a doctor on the matter."[10] Though the main figures in the movement never advocate abandonment of medical care (see chapter five), those who hear that healing is available to all who will claim it by faith might easily infer that. Many individuals have taken this step, some of them at the wrong time. As a result, Hobart Freeman has not had a total monopoly on tragic deaths brought on by rash presumption of faith.

Perhaps the best-known obituary within the faith movement is that of eleven-year-old diabetic Wesley Parker. His parents followed a familiar pattern—attending a revival meeting with strong faith, they laid claim to Isaiah 53 as a promise for their son. They also threw away his insulin and stood firm longer than most people do. Refusing to return to a doctor, they watched Wesley die in agony and even scheduled a resurrection service instead of a funeral. After the service Wesley was buried and the parents were arrested and jailed for child abuse.[11]

At least the Parkers somehow kept their faith in God. Amidst such disillusionment, however, apostasy can follow close behind. One man, for example, told me of his friend who was a close follower of a prominent local faith teacher in his southeastern city. When the teacher died of an untreated illness, this follower, overcome with despair, quit attending church.

Stories of healings and nonhealings get most of the attention, but exaggerated promises of prosperity have had equally frightening effects. In one case a couple with four children answered an evangelist's call to give sacrificially by donating much-needed funds.

For a month they existed on oatmeal until another pay check arrived. Unfortunately a layoff came the next month, and both the house and the car, which were nearly paid for, were repossessed. The pastor consoled them with the thought that probably they had not given with the right attitude. It was their fault, not the Lord's. . . . Although they remained in the church, the hurt remains in their hearts until today. They felt that the main lesson that God had taught them was never to trust a minister again.[12]

Meanwhile, abuses of positive confession can cause crippling psychological damage, as claiming a blessing or "speaking to" a problem becomes a replacement for dealing responsibly with life. Fred Price recounts instances of married couples using positive confession as their means of birth control, and then wondering what went wrong when a pregnancy occurred.[13] In a reverse case, one pastor and his wife, who were unable to have a baby, were told by a member of their church that they needed to "confess" a pregnancy and display their faith by purchasing a baby stroller and walking down the street with it!

A Pentecostal campus minister told me of a woman, influenced by positive-confession teaching, who attended his group one year. She became convinced that she was called to spend the summer ministering in China, even though she had little money and no knowledge of Chinese. God would enable her to learn the language in two months, she repeatedly confessed. She never ended up in China, and she later traded her Christian commitment for sorority involvement. All respectable faith teachers would quickly deny any intent to foster such unreasonable behavior, yet this woman received her initial inspiration from them.

Extreme forms of positive confession have also caused some followers to think they are in sin if for a moment they stop claiming victory. One woman who attends a faith church in the Midwest has pinpointed the dangers: "The picture I get is that as a Christian, I am supposed to be victorious all the time. I may be in pain, physically or mentally, but I must keep up my positive confession at all costs. This leads to superficial people with pious masks who cannot disclose to each other who they really are, and therefore cannot experience the grace of God where they hurt. They present their ideal rather than their real self. It's boring, and phony."

Episodes and experiences like the ones I have here retold are all too prevalent and frightful to be ignored. On the contrary, they ought to be more widely publicized, as a caution to overly zealous Christians seeking a big challenge to prove their faith.

Faith Teaching in Balance

But many of the writers and speakers retelling these stories and broadcasting these warnings have had little opportunity to interact with faith people who have chosen the more moderate response to our original dilemma, recognizing that God can work in many different ways. And so they have not seen such sights as a greeter standing at the door of a faith church, unashamedly displaying a bandage on a thumb that was injured at his job and would need several weeks to heal. They have not spoken with Christians who live simple lifestyles, listen regularly to Kenneth Copeland tapes, and see no contradiction between those two activities. They have not witnessed, it seems, the behavior of the many Christians who have applied faith teachings to their lives in a balanced manner. While often unnoticed, since their moderation is less newsworthy than either large healing crusades or pitiful tragedies, many followers of the faith message have chosen not to make reality conform to an inflexible theology but to temper their theology with common sense.

These faith people joyfully report that healings do take place in their church but recognize that instant miracles are not the usual result of prayer. They believe that God does want to heal, but they are keenly aware of the need for compassion and wisdom in dealing with the sick. They stress that faith can achieve great things, but they humbly acknowledge that they do not have all the answers to the mysteries of healing.

One faith pastor, expressing his concern for extremes that place too much responsibility on the people who are seeking healing or on a minister who is praying for the sick, told me: "Jesus is the healer, we stand on the Word, and we're not opposed to doctors." When people not healed through prayer come to him, he is quick to affirm their faith, lest they begin to feel inadequate and fall under condemnation.

Another experienced Christian, who has attended one of the

large Tulsa faith churches for two years, reports that the church encourages people to use all available methods of healing and that the pastor's wife has given birth to her children in a hospital. "We pray for the sick, but have no feeling of condescension toward those who go to the hospital," he says.

For these people, prosperity seems to be still less of a problem. Several of the faith pastors with whom I have communicated were quick to point out that the financial blessings we obtain are for God's sake, not ours. One of them, who like so many critics dismissed the faith teachings as self-oriented when he first heard them, later realized that he had not heard the whole message. "Prosperity is not for one's own personal gain," he stresses, "but to enable one to give more, support the gospel more, and do more in this world system that is run with money."

Another couple faced financial uncertainties due to unemployment during their first year in a faith church. After a full year both of them finally found steady work, just before their savings ran out. In the meantime, though, all their needs were met, and it never occurred to them to demand more than that of God. On the contrary, the faith message was imparting the knowledge that they did not have to worry but could trust God to always take care of them.

Bob Walker, now on the counseling staff of a faith ministry in Tulsa, has special insight in this area, having worked for Kenneth Hagin Ministries during his second year as a Rhema Bible School student. People forget, he points out, that Hagin and many other leaders in the faith movement toiled in less financially rewarding ministry for years or even decades before rising to their current stature. His own exposure to the faith movement's best-known figures was quickly counterbalanced when he graduated and took his first job, where he considered himself quite well compensated even though his salary was not likely to make him rich. Nearly all Rhema graduates need to be prepared, like Walker, to begin their ministry careers in small churches with unimpressive salaries, and the great majority of them seem ready to do just that to spread the gospel. In many cases they may actually be more ready to make such a sacrifice than other young pastors, due to their utter confidence that their needs will be met.

The concept of positive confession, when grounded and balanced, can also have practical benefit in helping struggling Christians know the victorious living that Christ has made available to us. The midwestern woman whose concerns with positive confession were noted earlier in this chapter has also told me that the faith message helped her end five years of struggling to live in victory over trials. Even Jimmy Swaggart admits that the faith message was instrumental in reviving his spirits during a time of discouragement, long before his ministry expanded to worldwide proportions.[14] Other pastors have noted that they joined forces with the faith ministries because the words of Hagin or Copeland enabled them to stop doubting and start believing that God wanted to put their gifts to use.

A Model Practitioner of Faith Teaching

My sample is certainly not statistically reliable, since a researcher requesting assistance is much more likely to receive help from a balanced than from an unbalanced Christian, but it shows that listening to the faith message has not proved to be universally hazardous to the hearers' spiritual health. Almost every adherent with whom I have spoken has freely acknowledged the existence of "bad apples" who have scarred the faith movement's reputation; several have expressed sympathy with the movement's critics and have been acting to correct some of the same errors those critics have spotted. Perhaps none of them represent a more complete testimony to this movement's value to contemporary Christianity than does Mark Moder, who graduated from Rhema Bible Training Center in 1982 and has since worked as a pastor in Maryland and Pittsburgh.

Moder became a Christian in 1977, while still in high school. He was introduced to the faith message and found that it enabled him to know the Bible as an exciting, life-giving reality. So when he felt a call to become a pastor, he decided to enroll at Rhema.

When he moved to Tulsa, he left everything, coming to a new city with few possessions and no job. He worked his way through school, living with two classmates and sleeping on just a mattress, for lack of a bed. This was not a serious concern for Mark, because his primary purpose for being there was to learn from God's Word—working just enough to supply his financial needs. The main thrust of the curriculum at Rhema, he found, was to win the world for Christ, not positive confession or prosperity.

Since leaving Tulsa, Moder and his wife (also a Rhema graduate) have continued to face financial trials. But they also affirm that God has always met their needs. As for the hundredfold return to which, some faith teachers say, he was entitled in exchange for leaving everything, he says he has obtained it in ways more meaningful than dollars: "God gave me friends and joy that were a hundred times better than I had ever had."

Moder realizes that much of the extreme practice within the faith movement can be traced to extreme teaching from some pastors and preachers. In recent years, however, he has heard a fresh and frequent emphasis on giving. Although some individuals may still be guilty of extremism, he feels that the bulk of the movement is being restored to a balanced view of prosperity.

When he ministers to the sick, Moder first checks for obstacles, such as unbelief or unforgiveness, that may be hindering prayer. Sometimes the hindrance cannot be found, as in the case of one cancer victim to whom he ministered for months and who died nevertheless. But he has no difficulty accepting this fact: "I've had prayers go unanswered just like every Christian, but we're all learning and growing. And even if we do miss, there is no condemnation for those who are in Christ."

Positive confession, Moder says, has helped give him freedom from fear in both secular employment and his ministry. But he seems to have little trouble identifying and avoiding its excesses: "If it's not the will of God, it won't happen!" he declares.

Even though he agrees that Rhema could do a more complete job of teaching its students how to preach, Moder has developed a preaching style to which few could object. He displays concern for knowing the historical context of the passages he quotes, for following proper rules of interpretation, and for using the whole Bible, not just isolated texts that might support the faith message.

Moder's careful approach to Scripture has led him to the conclusion that the faith teachers have misinterpreted a few of their favorite texts. But this discovery has not stopped him from incorporating into his own thought those insights that do seem reliable. He has heard and internalized the Hagins' comment that one should not listen to faith teachers only, since their work is not comprehensive (Hagin, for example, feels a special call to teach on faith, Copeland on prosperity). "We must learn from all the ministries," Moder concludes. By doing just that he has remained well-rounded in his Christian walk. In fact, he prefers not to be called a faith teacher but simply a Bible teacher, because he would like to see unity replace division among various groups of Christians—and because many pastors expect the worst as soon as they hear that he attended Rhema.

Social and Economic Pressures
All this commendable, mature wisdom comes from a young man whose only formal training took place on Kenneth Hagin's property. Moreover, Moder's sacrificial commitment to

furthering God's kingdom is far from unique among Rhema graduates. This fact brings us back to the question posed early in this chapter: why such variance from stability to selfishness within the faith movement? The answer lies, I believe, in the sociological dynamics that push the main faith teachers in two opposing directions and produce crossed doctrinal signals.

On one hand, Hagin and Copeland are at the head of a network of churches whose proceedings usually do not differ noticeably from those at other charismatic churches. A typical worship service includes Scripture songs and choruses (which have replaced traditional hymns), periods of corporate praise to God, a musical solo, announcements, an offering and a sermon. Only the common practice, in keeping with the emphasis on spoken confessions, of echoed prayers or statements of faith (with the congregation repeating the pastor's words, one phrase at a time) would distinguish most faith churches from other charismatic fellowships in style of worship. The sermons tend to be long and of a somewhat rambling character, but no more so than is commonly the case in other charismatic or Pentecostal churches, where the message's intent is normally to exhort and encourage more than to uncover the fine points of a biblical text.

On the other hand, thousands of followers are attracted to Hagin or Savelle or Capps precisely because of the teachings in which they specialize: healing, prosperity and positive confession. If these ministries decreased or softened their distinctives, they would no longer stand out from the growing throng of independent charismatic ministries and would risk losing much of their devoted following. It is those consistent followers—including some bad apples—whose contributions support the ministries' multimillion-dollar budgets.

These factors explain, for example, how Kenneth Copeland can display an understanding of the many-faceted biblical view of prosperity and yet place such an overwhelming emphasis on its financial aspect. For in the high-pressure atmosphere of an international ministry, Copeland faces a natural temptation with which nearly every local pastor can sympathize—the tendency to preach what one's supporters want to hear. Sermons challenging people to seek spiritual prosperity so as to meet the needs of others seldom draw huge audiences; motivational talks offering the key to wealth do. Copeland knows and preaches about many other aspects of the Christian life, but his message that God wills financial prosperity is the one most attractive to his large, loyal following. If he wants his ministry to continue expanding, he can hardly downplay that message now. Despite the criticism he has received from some corners, he has decided, not surprisingly, to give it more attention in the future.[15]

Hagin, Jr., has discussed this very problem of listeners who insist on hearing only "what their itching ears want to hear" (2 Tim 4:3). He notes that miracle healings and other spectacular manifestations attract more notice than does solid teaching on how to worship and serve God, since most people "prefer getting involved with the spectacular—with something in the emotional realm—instead of getting involved with God in our spirits."[16] They want to hear about health, wealth and miracles and will pay both attention and contributions to those teachers who entertain and excite them by centering on these subjects.

As we saw throughout our analysis of the main theological issues (chapters five, six and seven), the Hagins, the Copelands, Savelle and Price all have repudiated abuses in the faith movement and have made explicit calls for more balanced behavior. All six of these leaders seem to be honest, sincere Christians, and so they naturally feel a strong urge to speak out against error when they see it tarnishing followers' lives and their Christian witness. Yet the opposite urge, pushing them to teach on those subjects that keep the ministry rolling, is just as strong. When prominent evangelists develop popularity based on favorite teachings, it is far easier to continue in that direction than to move against the stream of popular demand toward greater balance.

The economics of America's independent parachurch media ministries makes going against the current even harder. Many well-known faith teachers do not pastor a church of their own, so they have no list of members whose donations they can count on receiving consistently. If they do not continue to successfully solicit contributions and sell their books and tapes, they have no guaranteed income against which to borrow. Their only alternative is to go into debt or quickly curtail their work. As Christian sociologist Os Guinness has observed, "Almost anything can be said on commercial TV, *but only if someone can afford to say it and if one can say it profitably.*"[7] So those itching ears will continue to be tickled by evangelists who, even if sincere in their Christian motivation, know that they need to keep the itching ears tickled lest the checks stop coming and their ministries suffer as a result.

Some of the practices faith ministries use in seeking financial support have, in fact, caused some observers to wonder if these preachers really believe what they teach about trusting in God for prosperity. In this regard Fred Price stands out as an admirable model: on his television program, he keeps his requests for money noticeably brief and low-key, and he has described faith ministries that beg for offerings as "pitiful."[18] Others, though, seem to see no contradiction between trusting God and pleading for contributions. Several leading faith teachers use regular direct mailings in search of donations. And on one night of Bob Tilton's "Holy Ghost God-sent miracle revival," transmitted nationally by satellite in spring 1985, his appeal for money lasted longer than the sermon.

Jerry Savelle, in one service recorded for cable television and designed to help raise money for Copeland's proposed World Outreach Headquarters building in Fort Worth, invoked a literal application of the hundredfold return in an unusual and potentially exploitative manner. With a live audience watching, Savelle handed Copeland ten checks for one thousand dollars each and stated:

> Each of these $1,000 checks I am now giving to you will return one hundredfold to me, according to God's Word. One for my church, one for my school, one for my mission work, . . . and this last one for my wife and myself personally. Folks, these checks will return a total of $100,000 each! Can you say "Praise the Lord"? What are you waiting for? Get on your feet and get in on this! Let's take the biggest offering ever! I want it now! Who will do what I did? Who will sow in famine and reap one hundredfold? Well, come on! Come running, you sower![19]

While I understand the financial needs of international Christian outreaches, I fear that sales pitches like this one are only setting the stage for massive heartbreak and disillusionment.

The ministries' financial needs may be related to another practice that serves to increase the danger of extremism: their ceaseless production and marketing of new releases, often with highly repetitive content. Sometimes the faith teachers use not only the same Scriptures and arguments in more than one book, but even the same anecdotes.[20] These teachers should not be criticized for focusing on some aspects of Christian truth while omitting others, since they should be allowed to specialize in faith just as Billy Graham centers on salvation and James Dobson on family issues. What does cause concern, though, is their implicit willingness to become the sole source of spiritual food for a substantial sector of American Christianity. Hagin, Jr., has said that no one should listen only to faith teachers,[21] but the many devoted adherents who regularly buy the newest materials from Hagin, Copeland or Savelle to keep their "faith library" up to date probably have little money left in their budgets for books by other authors.

The proliferation of faith churches threatens to compound the problem still further, as thousands of charismatic Christians are drawn away from more reputable churches and into fellowships where the pastor has little or no theological education, receives most of his own input and inspiration from the faith movement and is thus unprepared to guide his flock by the whole counsel of God. If the movement continues in this direction, it will produce a horde of believers full of faith for healing but largely ignorant of biblical principles regarding parenting, marriage, social and ethical issues, and many other important areas of Christian living.

Much of the faith message is potentially valuable, but *not* when isolated from the rest of sound Christian doctrine. Much more interaction between faith teachers and other Christian ministries is needed. As we have seen, there are several prominent faith teachers and many of their followers who are distraught over their movement's excesses. Perhaps they will awaken to the ways in which they inadvertently sow confusion along with truth.

Although there are exceptions (Hobart Freeman's damage occurred mostly in northern Indiana), the potential danger of the faith message has increased significantly in the South, more so than in the North (or anywhere else in the world). Many northern cities have just one or two small faith churches. Their pastors would be isolated and ignored if they did not interact with other local church leaders. This interaction keeps them aware of the full range of biblical concerns. Furthermore, a large percentage of the individuals who read or listen to Hagin and Copeland in the North are still attending churches not tied to the faith movement, so that the teaching they receive in their own churches helps them maintain a more balanced Christian walk. By contrast, in cities like Tulsa and Dallas, where numerous faith churches boast a combined membership of many thousands, there is plenty of camaraderie and contacts with Christians outside the movement can dissolve more easily. And, since the biggest success stories tend to draw the biggest crowds, a can-you-top-this mentality can begin to take hold. As a result, the same extreme teachings and practices that would usually stymie a church's growth in the North become strategically advantageous in the South.

For a variety of reasons, then, the same faith message can be inspiring for Pastor Mark Moder in Pittsburgh and an unmitigated disaster for Pastor Ben Byrd in Columbia, South Carolina.[22]

Errors and Lessons

Byrd was a discouraged Southern Baptist ex-pastor who re-entered the ministry after receiving "baptism in the Spirit." The friend who had led him into this charismatic experience also introduced him to the work of Hagin, Copeland, Capps and other faith teachers. Believing that God wanted to heal and deliver people from bondage, Byrd was attracted by the faith teachers' commitment to affirm and appropriate God's power. He began to study their materials with enthusiasm. "I probably kept some of these ministries in business by the number of tapes I ordered," he recalls. "I immediately began to see some things that seemed to contradict what I had learned as a Baptist and serious Bible student, but I thought that surely these people knew more than I did because of the size of their ministries. So I believed, without fully agreeing with, some of these things."

Byrd became heavily involved with the movement, personally meeting some of its leaders and purchasing a satellite dish for his church so that he could receive Bob Tilton's programming. He served as administrator in his area for Copeland's satellite world communion service. The more he learned, though, the more he wondered.

His period of questioning began when one Texas pastor, a

close friend of one of the movement's best-known figures, discussed successful forms of ministry and explained, in Byrd's words, "the procedure that was most effective in manipulating people." As Byrd attended the faith conventions he noticed that the speakers tended to use and re-use a handful of Bible passages as their texts, usually, he felt, taking them out of their proper context. Just as disturbingly, he heard the same people repeat the same prophecies, or the same message in tongues and interpretation, at two different meetings. Twice in one year he heard the same man tell convention gatherings that "God told me" to take a special offering to meet a desperate need the Copelands were experiencing.

When Byrd expressed his uneasiness to some of his closest friends within the faith movement, they replied that they too had seen problems. But, they answered, "This is the hottest thing going, and we're not going to say anything bad about it." When he heard what he considered serious cases of false teaching, however, Byrd felt he could no longer remain silent. When he called the headquarters of the faith ministry spreading the teachings, a worker there told him that the staff knew errors had been taught but felt they had to give the people what they wanted. God, they felt, could meet the needs of searching listeners even if they were attracted to the satellite services by questionable teaching. Byrd told them that they were, in effect, lying to their audience. The response was, "We don't call it lying. We feel that it's a positive influence."

Byrd was in attendance at the Charlotte, North Carolina, convention in 1981 on the evening when Savelle unexpectedly replaced Copeland at the pulpit, and announced that he had received a visit from Jesus in his motel room that afternoon. He then launched into his just-obtained message on "sowing in famine"—that is, giving generously even when one is short on money. Of Savelle's lengthy sermon that night, Byrd says, "It was the most emotional thing I've ever heard." He recalls that the listeners were told to give sacrificially, beyond their capabilities, and trust that they would receive a hundredfold return within a year.[23] Some of the people who contributed large amounts of money and possessions that night were members of his church. So Byrd saw firsthand the suffering they went through when the promised return failed to materialize. In these cases and others, he laments, he has seen extreme versions of the prosperity message leave unsuspecting believers "spiritually raped."

In an attempt to reduce such painful occurrences among the churches in Columbia, Byrd invited the area's other faith pastors to his home for dinner and shared what he had seen and learned with them. He did not achieve his intent, however, as his guests became upset and soon cut off their relationships with him.

While he has no desire to "sling mud," Byrd feels God allowed him to have these experiences and gain inside knowledge of the movement so that he could serve as a spokesman helping others to avoid making the same mistakes. Since he openly repented to his congregation in 1982 for his involvement in the movement, he has spoken out against its abuses in churches throughout the eastern part of the country. He feels that the faith teachers started out with good intentions but that, when some of their misinterpretations (especially those on prosperity) became popular, "their ministries grew so fast that it shocked them, and they have been forced, by their own greed or by their business advisors, to keep this thing going." What he has seen in the faith movement reminds him all too well of the ancient church of Laodicea, as described in the book of Revelation: it thinks itself to be "rich" but is actually "poor, blind and naked" (Rev 3:17).[24]

Byrd's story leaves little doubt that, at least on occasion, some faith teachers have succumbed to the pressures that come with the enormous responsibility of their role as prominent Christian evangelists. Before we become judgmental, though, we would do well to recall the familiar proverb that one should not criticize another person until he or she has walked in that person's moccasins. The moccasins of the faith teachers, like those of all influential evangelists, are big ones, shoes that I certainly would not want to have to fill. Just as we did not outlaw the Republican party after President Nixon was impeached, so we must exercise careful discernment in judging this movement that has positively transformed many lives and ruined others. Because the stakes are so high—the potential benefits and sufferings both so great—the effort is necessary.

TEN

Seeing What Is Really There

THERE ONCE LIVED A MAN WHO HAD A WAY OF STIRRING up trouble wherever he went. He didn't mean any harm—he actually thought that everyone else was at fault. Nobody knew where he had come from, but everyone knew that wherever he went, trouble was sure to follow.

It all started on his first Sunday in church—at least the first Sunday anyone noticed him (newcomers often go unnoticed unless they do something unusual). When it came time for the Scripture reading, he missed hearing what verses would be read, so he looked over his neighbor's shoulder. As he did so, he saw a solid black line running through several verses of his neighbor's Bible.

"Why did you do that?" our man exclaimed.

"Do what?"

"Cross out those verses in your Bible! Don't you believe in following the whole counsel of God?"

"I don't know what you're talking about. I haven't crossed out anything."

The two men never managed to agree on what had been crossed out. Our friend went home disgusted, but proud that he could see God's complete will better than his neighbor could.

This incident passed quietly, but the next one did not. A few Sundays later, when the time for the choral anthem arrived, the man noticed that the song was a familiar one—a Bach four-part chorale that he had sung as a youngster. With head tilted and nose protruding upward, he examined the choir. There was a well-attired contingent of sopranos and altos, along with several basses; but where there should have been tenors, he saw only a dark, empty pew. Amazed at the choir director's oversight, he could not concentrate on the anthem. After the service he bluntly rebuked the choir director.

"What do you mean?" the director responded. "We had four tenors in the back left pew."

"No way!" declared the man. "That's exactly where I looked, and there was nobody."

He appealed to a few bystanders for their support, but all of them said that they had either dozed off during the anthem or had seen several men in the back left choir pew. So he went home frustrated, but convinced that he was more alert and attentive than the other church members.

These and other episodes left everyone on edge. Nerves frayed and tension rose whenever he was around. The spirit of the whole church was poisoned, and the leaders decided that the only feasible solution was to get rid of him. So they instructed everyone to ignore him or treat him miserably. After a few weeks he got the message and left.

He went to a second church where much the same thing happened, and then to a third.

In his fourth church a compassionate elder, having heard the stories from the other three congregations, determined not to give up until he had gotten to the root of the problem. He asked the man to come in for a counseling session. "Sure, I'll come," the man said, "because I hope sooner or later someone will realize that I'm the one seeing things clearly and all of you are the wackos."

The session was already deteriorating when suddenly our man interrupted, "By the way, Mr. Elder, you shouldn't be wearing a suit coat with a big ugly smudge on it."

"Where?" the elder asked.

"In the middle of your left lapel. Don't you see it?"

"No. I don't see a thing. I just had the coat dry-cleaned. Maybe the shadow is affecting you."

"No way!" the man insisted. "It's as black as can be! I don't see how you can miss it."

The man went home frustrated again, but thankful to God that he didn't have blind spots like everyone else. The elder, meanwhile, was convinced that this man was either schizophrenic or hallucinatory. But he wanted to keep the man in the church, in the hope that the pastor's preaching would somehow have an effect on him.

The elder, who also happened to be an eye doctor, finally hit upon an idea. If he could convince the man to wear thick glasses, people would think he was a senior citizen. And then more people would be willing to put up with him. After all, many church members, thinking that all elderly persons are senile, only pretend to listen to them without paying the least bit of attention to what they are saying.

The elder managed to get the man to come in for an eye exam. As he gave the exam, he was surprised to discover that the man kept leaving out a letter or two in each line he read with his left eye.

"Are you leaving out those letters on purpose?" he asked.

"No, I'm not leaving out any letters."

The doctor turned on his flashlight to take a closer look at the eye. After a few moments, he spotted a tiny sliver lodged in the eyeball. Sometimes, when the man blinked, the sliver would begin to float around inside the eye, then become stuck in one place and remain there.

"How long have you had that sliver in your eye?" he asked.

"I don't *have* a sliver in my eye."

"Come on now, it must hurt your eye occasionally. It looks like a microscopic two-by-four knocking around in the eyeball."

"I don't know anything about it."

The man insisted he had nothing in his eye. But since the elder had been so kind he agreed to some exploratory surgery. The sliver was surgically removed, and with it the man's judgmental behavior.

Too many of us, like this man, are willing to look for imperfections everywhere but within ourselves. Many of us have treated the faith message in just this way, publicizing its errors and excesses but unwilling to notice what faith teachers may have to offer us.

Some Positive Benefits

Take the faith movement's emphasis on "getting into the Word," for example. In healthy contrast to some modern teachers, especially within the charismatic renewal, who have taught Christians to receive personal guidance primarily from their "shepherds" or spiritual leaders, the faith movement strongly encourages its people to seek their own guidance directly from the Lord. The faith teachers speak of the reality of the Holy Spirit within every believer, even in those who do not believe in the Pentecostal baptism in the Spirit.[1]

Some Christians talk as if they want to receive their instruction from pastors steeped in biblical and theological training, rather than from personal study. Solid training is important for pastors, of course, and no one should begin expounding a new doctrine without first seeking the counsel and insight of other mature believers. But the example of the early church suggests that unschooled fishermen and tax collectors can become teachers simply by sitting at the feet of the Master.

Even a Christian psychology professor who analyzed the faith movement's attitude toward illness and cure was struck by these teachers' unusually deep and direct dependence on the power of the Scriptures. "All of the teachers' techniques," he commented, "appear calculated to build the Word of God firmly into the believer's consciousness. Theoretically, then, in times of trouble or need, the believers will trust more in what the Scriptures say and less in their sense knowledge."[2] In the spirit of Psalm 119 the faith teachers praise God for the privilege of being instructed and strengthened by meditating on his Word, setting an example for many twentieth-century Christians.

Second, the faith teachers take seriously the existence of Satan, our enemy, as well as the power of our victorious Lord. Some of their methods of spiritual warfare may seem bizarre, even infantile: the act of audibly laughing at the devil in a public meeting sounds inappropriate for adults, and Hagin and Copeland's supposed conversations with Satan seem best suited for either a morality play or a book of children's stories. Such conversations, though, have ample biblical precedent,[3] and even my own experiences while performing this research have illustrated the effectiveness of this approach. When tempted to sulk in discouragement, or to neglect prayer, I have found myself instinctively remembering that this is Satan's desire for me. This awareness has often renewed my vigor and discipline as I proceed with a chuckle to continue in what I know God wants me to do.[4]

Third, whatever one thinks of their theology, the fact remains that these evangelists are trying to build up the faith of their listeners, and for that they have biblical precedent. Today's church seeks to increase its members' knowledge, social concern and financial contributions. All of these are good. But more often than not, we forget the urgent request of the apostles. "Increase our faith!" they begged (Lk 17:5). They knew the power of faith. They remembered the demon they should have expelled but could not. They wanted all the power that was available to them, even if they had no systematic theology of the Holy Spirit.

Today the power of faith in God is often forgotten. Pastors commendably arouse Christians to good works, while simultaneously affirming that salvation is by faith alone. They willingly embrace both sides of this apparent paradox—faith and works. But many of them are unwilling to embrace both boldness in prayer and God's sovereignty, arguing instead that anyone whose prayers sound bold and demanding has "put God in a box." Clearly, this boldness can be grossly misused by people guilty of false motives or false doctrine. Nevertheless, the bulk of scriptural prayer is noticeably bold, and sometimes, as in the case of Peter and the crippled beggar, prayer actually becomes a command: "In the name of Jesus . . . walk" (Acts 3:6).

I have no problem with praying in faith for physical and material blessings—as long as the kingdom of God is always retained as one's ultimate purpose and first priority. On this note I turn to what I hope will be interpreted by all readers as constructive criticism.

If we study the faith literature we will find all the elements needed to give the movement proper balance. Kenneth Hagin admits that sometimes we just don't know why people are not healed. He and his colleagues approve of medical science. They warn against seeking riches for their own sake. The problem is simply that they do not say these things *often enough*. This is not the message that most faith people are anxious to hear. And for that very reason it needs to be stated *more often* than those parts of the faith message that we humans, in our weakness, are itching to hear.

We want a painless Christianity—"cheap grace," in the immortal words of German martyr Dietrich Bonhoeffer.[5] We want to have perfect health and the "American dream." We do not want to have to deny ourselves and deal with suffering. Because we naturally tend toward gratifying the flesh, faith teachers and their followers everywhere need to talk more about God's sovereign lordship over our lives. We need more reminders that God is the potter and we are the clay; more teaching on how to show real compassion for those who are hurting, physically or otherwise; more insistence on the central fact that lasting contentment lies in finding God's will for one's life, not in an upper-middle-class income. Faith teachers have said these things, but further steps must be taken to correct the self-centeredness of those who have heard only what they want to hear—salvation and blessings—and are putting the gospel of Christ to shame.

While some of the faith teachers' statements have been used by followers in a way that limits God's sovereignty, I am not convinced that the mainstream of the faith movement is heretical on any specific point. Thus my primary objection is not to any particular doctrine but to the way in which the faith teachers read and use the Bible. Their method of interpretation (if indeed it can be called a method) is such that one can never be fully sure what they will say next. Although Kenneth Hagin, whose message has remained constant through fifty years of ministry, is not likely to fall into serious error, other teachers inspired by faith teachings have done so. And if they continue to do so, the strange doctrinal innovations that have ripped apart the seams of Pentecostalism throughout the century will do the same to the faith movement. The faith movement must begin to teach proper principles of Bible study and interpretation.[6]

The following four sections are intended as first steps toward more responsible biblical study (a step from which all of us could benefit) and toward refinement of the faith teachers' approach to healing, prosperity and positive confession.

Hermeneutics—a Long but Necessary Word

As a former college soccer player, I sometimes pull my cleats out of mothballs and coach youngsters. On one occasion I was demonstrating when it is legal in soccer to push an opponent with the shoulder. "First you have to be beside the other player and near the ball," I explained. "And you must shove him shoulder to shoulder. Then even if he falls down it's perfectly legal."

A few days later, on my way home from work, I came upon a commotion at the subway station. Several policemen were on the scene, and as I approached I was shocked to discover that the boy wearing handcuffs was one of my soccer players.

When I asked him how he had gotten into this predicament, he eagerly replied, "I did just what you told us, and they're locking me up for assault!"

"What are you talking about?" I inquired, more stunned than before.

"I can quote your exact words: 'You must shove him shoulder to shoulder. Then even if he falls down it's perfectly legal.' So that's what I did, trying to catch the subway, and one guy almost fell into the tracks so they arrested me!"

It should be obvious by now that my friend had taken my words out of their original context (the soccer field) and applied them to a new context (the subway). He had violated the intent of my statement. Why is it not equally obvious to thousands of gullible Christians that when a Bible teacher takes, for instance, Proverbs 6:2 ("Thou art snared with the words of thy mouth" KJV) out of its original context (an unwise financial agreement) and applies the verse indiscriminately to everything we speak, he is misinterpreting God's Word?

To avoid such errors we need not just exegesis (the science of figuring out just what the author of a given biblical text meant) but also hermeneutics (which, building on exegesis, investigates how we might apply that text to life today). Hermeneutics teaches us how to interpret Scripture in light of the writer's situation, other passages of Scripture and basic principles of interpretation. It is the antidote to proof-texting—grabbing verses of the Bible as if they can be read without regard for either their setting or common sense.

Bad hermeneutics represents a far greater cause for concern than any specific doctrinal deviation. Since everyone has blind spots, a degree of tolerance makes fellowship possible among Christians who disagree on issues not essential to salvation. As long as they accept the Bible's authority and employ proper principles of interpretation, one can be confident that they will not err in areas where the Bible's position is unmistakable (such as the resurrection and the need to accept Jesus as Savior and Lord). But when a teacher interprets the Bible whimsically, ignoring proper hermeneutics—as the faith teachers sometimes appear to do—there remains no control to assure that his or her next message will not go wildly astray. Like John Alexander Dowie in 1900, the teacher might declare himself the reincarnation of Elijah; or, like Hobart Freeman in 1970 and Dowie before him, he might begin to preach that doctors are of the devil; or, like some of Paul's enemies in the first century, he might claim that the final resurrection has already happened.[7] It may seem inconceivable that veteran teachers like Hagin and Copeland could ever end up in gross error; but who ever thought that Hobart Freeman would turn out as he did?

Nowhere in contemporary Christianity is sound biblical interpretation so desperately needed as within charismatic circles. Consumed with a hunger to see congregations overflow with the spirit of praise, charismatics have made great strides in the area of worship. But often, especially in the independent and nondenominational churches, their valid concern for a religion of the heart has unseated reliable teaching and Bible study from its central position in any body of believers. There is no option or substitute: Serious, consistent, contextual Bible study is essential for any church that wishes to stay on the narrow path of godliness. Flimsy or out-of-context treatment of the Word of God must not be tolerated.

The sociology of the charismatic movement underscores its desperate need for a clear summons to sound Bible study and teaching. Because of the charismatics' strong accent on worship, their Sunday morning services have outgrown and sometimes doubled the traditional length of one hour. Since few people are anxious to spend three hours or more in church each Sunday morning, adult Bible classes are nonexistent or poorly attended. Furthermore, charismatic churches, attracted as they are to religious experience, often value entertainment more than careful exposition in their pastors' preaching. Judging from their sermons, many charismatic pastors seem to be better trained in theatrics than in hermeneutics.

All of this results in churches that call the Bible the Word of God and regularly search the Scriptures for proof texts but offer no effective, reliable teaching whatsoever. These churches may at first appear biblically based, but in actuality their sermons and study groups use the Bible in a careless, selective or incomplete manner. More often than not, the churches that are subject to this trend are reaping the fruits of their practice: members base important life decisions on doubtful Bible interpretations picked up uncritically from favorite television evangelists.

This doesn't mean that only veteran scholars with theological backgrounds can safely study or teach Scripture. The lay members of the church are capable of personal study and teaching, but they should take certain precautions. It is unwise, for example, to base any teaching on a single passage of Scripture. Clearer passages can be used to help explain more difficult ones. Before claiming to have discovered any new revelation, one should seek counsel and discernment from pastors, elders or Christians who have done advanced study. Accountability among Christians often nips budding heresy before it can take root and spread, while people who arrogantly refuse to listen to others quickly slide into error.[8]

Christians should expect a firm commitment to proper study from their pastors and teachers, should examine all teaching in the light of Scripture, should beware of bad hermeneutics, and should lovingly approach their teachers when they suspect questionable biblical interpretation in their church. A concern for the purity of the gospel is every Christian's responsibility.[9]

Faith without Guilt: Fine-Tuning the Gospel of Healing

It is possible to teach and practice a powerful ministry of healing without engaging in the more dubious expressions of positive confession, such as denial of symptoms. And without causing the chronically sick to lose heart. The controversy over the faith movement has obscured this fact. Some of the best instruction within the modern charismatic renewal has come from Dennis Bennett, whose quarter-century of charismatic ministry within a mainline (Episcopal) church has ripened into a ministry of faith and mature moderation. While his ministry parallels the faith message in some respects, there are also noteworthy differences.

Bennett insists that it is always God's will to heal and that it is important for people needing healing to seek ways to build up their faith. He is sympathetic to the faith movement, recognizing the force of spoken faith (as in Mark 11:22-23) and positive thinking. But he categorically refuses to tell a sick Christian that he or she is lacking in faith. Since Jesus healed in answer to the prayer of "I believe; help my unbelief," Bennett finds it adequate, when praying for the sick, to ask not if they *will* be healed immediately but "Do you believe Jesus *can* do this thing?"[10]

The barriers to healing, says Bennett, are always on our side, not God's, but this fact should not be a cause for guilt or proof that the unhealed are harboring some "secret sin." In some cases sickness may be the result of "a deeply hidden problem which [the sick person] as yet has no way to unearth." Therefore that person ought to investigate any new spiritual insights or approaches that might remove the barriers, just as one would try newly developed medical procedures even if previous therapies had failed. If these efforts still do not work, the person need not feel discouraged, because "It isn't his fault and it isn't God's fault."[11]

Though he stresses that "only our faith opens the way for [God] to help us," Bennett articulates the nature of faith in such a way as to avoid producing guilt. Since faith is not a measurable quantity, he notes, to presume that someone "doesn't have enough faith" is nonsense. People should be encouraged to trust God for healing but must still recognize that, as inhabitants of a fallen world, we remain exposed daily to the devil's pervasive malice. We should always pray to the God of miracles, no matter how serious the situation. But denying medical assistance is definitely not the norm, and medications should not be discontinued until a doctor has confirmed the healing.[12]

Bennett maintains a positive, believing attitude toward God's miracle-working power but deals responsibly and compassionately with the many believers who wonder what went wrong when they were not healed. So does Francis MacNutt, who was a modern pioneer in healing ministry within the Catholic Church. His masterpiece *Healing* (1974) draws on his considerable firsthand experience. In this book MacNutt carefully and precisely distinguishes two categories of Christian healers: those who believe that "healing is ordinary and normative, but does not always take place," and those who teach basically that "healing always takes place if there is faith." He places himself in the former category and cites Hagin as an example of the latter approach. MacNutt concedes that in some cases God may inspire the sick to take the "risk of faith" and declare themselves healed, but insists that these instances are not the norm: "To say that this method is for *all* sick persons leads, I believe, to grave pastoral harm."[13]

MacNutt finds the phrase "if it be your will" as inappropriate as does any faith teacher, yet he is much more willing than they to include "failure" in his theology. "God's normative will is that people be healed, unless there is some countervailing reason," he states. But one of the reasons he offers is simply that "now is not the time." He admits that sometimes healings "do not seem to occur, at least on the physical level, at all." Despite the many miracles he has witnessed, he continues to affirm not his expertise in healing but his sense of how little he—like all of us—really knows: "Healing is mysterious. The best that man can do is to bow down before the mystery that is God."[14]

In this age when so many Protestant and independent charismatics act and speak as if they have mastered the "laws of faith," MacNutt aptly recalls a statement he heard from a Methodist scholar: "Protestants began by rejecting Catholicism for what they conceived was its reliance on works for salvation. But now, for some Protestants, faith has become the works they struggle to achieve."[15] Or, as one scholarly analyst has explained his preference for MacNutt's teaching over Hagin's: "In these two approaches, typified by these two men, you have a Protestant preaching law (in effect, at least) on the one hand, and a Catholic demonstrating grace on the other."[16]

Bennett and MacNutt's moderation can help to eliminate the anger, guilt feelings and broken hearts that faith teaching has sometimes (unintentionally) produced in those not healed. But, as we have seen, many faith adherents are quite capable of compassion and flexibility and, in practice, of ministering healing in a fashion not far removed from that of Bennett and MacNutt. It is hoped, then, that faith Christians can welcome the position I am advocating as a corrective to their healing ministry, not as an opposing view to be refuted.

Since most Christians believe that God *can* heal miraculously, and since most faith-message adherents are willing to grant that their healings often are delayed, I believe that understanding can be reached on common ground. That would cool dissension and greatly strengthen the whole church's ministry of healing. That common ground might be found in four symmetrical principles:

1a. God wants us to be healed. When we need healing we should ask God for it and trust him to answer.

1b. Physical healing does not always appear quickly in the sense realm. This fact implies that medicine should be welcomed and used, and that in some cases physical healing may actually be the ultimate healing—the obtaining of a glorified body through death.

2a. The sick should be encouraged to root out all possible obstacles to healing, including weakness of faith.

2b. If not noticeably healed, the sick should trust that God is working in them and should get on with their lives. If God reveals to them a new approach or a problem area in their lives, they should not hesitate to resume prayer for healing; if not, they should recognize their right to be free from guilt and to trust that God will use them just as they are.

Let us not focus so heavily on physical healing that we neglect or even hinder the many other, often more important, forms of healing—of souls, emotions, marriages, relationships—that God desires for us.[17]

A Theology of Prosperity: Fine-Tuning the Gospel of Wealth

Fred Price has stated, "If the Mafia can ride around in Lincoln Continental tour cars, why can't the King's kids?"[18] Statements like this one have naturally evoked the accusation that Price, the Copelands and others are diluting true Christianity by glorifying personal success and prosperity. But I think the prosperity people deserve more than a flippant answer. After all, those prized diamonds and fine cars are part of God's created world, and the Old Testament offers no apologies for the great personal wealth of Abraham, Joseph, Job and David. Nor have most of the Christians who decry Robert Schuller's Crystal Cathedral in California as wastefully extravagant ever felt a need to apologize for the opulence and architectural beauty of Europe's famous cathedrals (or of thousands of stately American church buildings). The issue of use and abuse of material wealth is more complex than some have tried to make it. These examples point to the need for a more comprehensive theology of prosperity.

Two biblical foils—two of the many negative examples Jesus used to highlight his teachings—provide a gateway to this quest. The first is a character whom we have seen before: the rich ruler of Mark 10. He liked his money. Jesus knew it, and so he pierced this wealthy man's heart with the command to give everything away. As the man's face dropped, Jesus declared for all to hear, "How hard it is for the rich to enter the kingdom of God!"

The second foil is also familiar: Judas. He watched angrily as Mary, whose brother Jesus had summoned back to life from the grave, "wasted" a pound of costly ointment on the Messiah's feet (Jn 12:1-8). Judas seemed convinced that the advice given to the rich ruler covered her case as well: sell your valuables and give the money away. Jesus, more willing to work on a case-by-case basis, shocked his onlookers by telling her she had done a fine thing.

These two episodes show that Jesus' view of wealth could be applied differently, depending on the individual situation. Both giving and spending can be appropriate. Instead of iron-clad regulations we must look for larger principles governing the use of money.

The first timeless principle is motivation. We must constantly be asking ourselves: Are we using the resources we have in the most servantlike way possible, seeking first the will of God for every dollar that passes through our hands?

A second important principle occupies a prominent position as the tenth commandment of Moses: "You shall not covet." What is our attitude toward those who possess what we lack? If we find ourselves falling into jealousy, or secretly wishing the tables somehow could be turned, we are exhibiting the symptoms of a deep and potentially ruinous spiritual problem.

These two principles have far-reaching applications to our daily lives, and to the current controversy between the apostles of success and the apostles of sacrifice. Both factions sometimes tend to forget the obvious fact that, to achieve his purposes, God uses both the prosperous and the poor. The God who wants all mankind to be saved, and who has chosen to use his people to reach the rest, can best reach the affluent of society through the ministry of affluent Christians. On the other hand, the Christian who tries to relate to the underprivileged while maintaining a luxurious suburban lifestyle will make little progress. A three-piece suit is a prerequisite to gaining a hearing from corporate executives, but for an inner-city preacher even the polished shoes must go.[19]

Amidst the warnings against setting one's heart on worldly things, a warning against the other extreme must be inserted. Some people decry nearly any unnecessary expenditures as improper stewardship; they do so usually with good intentions but with a false sense of what is genuinely practical. If God were as inflexibly practical as these Christians, he could overrule even the laws of nature and cause all his followers to survive without sleep, food, sex or winter clothing, so that the maximum of time and energy could be devoted to formal ministry. He does not do this. Instead the Lord has made life a wondrous gift to be abundantly enjoyed, not an endless string of duties and assignments. Legalistic insistence on maximum sacrifice is counterproductive and quenches inner peace and joy, in addition to failing to convince the unbelieving world that Christians really have something it needs.[20]

Since Jesus dealt with people and their possessions case by case, we must allow the Holy Spirit, working in people's consciences, to do the same today. If you sense a calling to mission work in a primitive land, accept it joyfully and do not pine for the comforts that you will miss. Do not envy those with larger incomes—for violating your conscience in pursuit of wealth will not make you happy. Rich persons who have turned away from God in climbing the economic ladder are to be pitied, not envied, for they have stored up treasures in the wrong place and will regret that decision in due time. Conversely, rich persons who have remained faithful to God while experiencing financial prosperity are entitled to enjoy their blessings, always remembering that more is expected from those to whom more is given, always seeking wholeheartedly the path that will best please God. The key goal is *detachment*—having our priorities straight so that our love for God dictates our use of material things rather than our material appetites dictating the intensity of our devotion to God.

My wife and I provide special weekend surprises for each other's birthdays. Thus, twice a year, we spend more than usual on ourselves, reaping the priceless fruit of a rejuvenated marriage relationship. Between special events, though, we might go for weeks without a frivolous expense, because, as we strive to see things through God's eyes instead of Madison Avenue's, we find no good reasons to spend. Similarly, we have one diamond to our name, and its visibility on Nancy's finger, challenging us always to treasure our commitment to each other, more than justifies its cost. But I can't imagine ever needing another one.

Yes, the diamonds and the Rolls Royces are part of a world that Christ has called us to redeem. But if we intently devote ourselves to the work of God's kingdom, we will be too busy— and too fulfilled—to worry about who has the diamonds.

A Theology of Complaining: Fine-Tuning Positive Confession

We have all known them—there never seems to be a shortage of them. They are hypochondriac, critic and pessimist all rolled into one. No matter how well things are going, they always seem to have something to complain about. Even worse, they seem to find a perverse joy in announcing their woes to all who will listen. Even those who do not care much for the positive confession teachings end up wishing they could invade these people's minds with a Charles Capps book—anything to silence their negativism that discourages everyone and does no one any good.

At the same time, we know that we need to be able to provide meaningful support for those who really are suffering. We know something is wrong when people are scared to say "I'm sick" or "I'm depressed," lest they be accused of making a wrong confession. People should feel welcome, even encouraged, to share their physical and spiritual needs, so that they can receive appropriate ministry and be restored to wholeness. Perhaps we need a theology of complaining to help us minister authentically to both the self-appointed martyrs and the bereaved, as well as to everyone in between.

The Scriptures are full of what some would call positive confessions (to avoid misunderstanding, I will call them positive Christian affirmations). In one of the most lavish and best-known promises, Paul assures us that everything works for good for God's people. Thanks to Christ, he proclaims, we are "more than conquerors." Through Christ, he boasts, "I can do everything." A more positive attitude can hardly be imagined.[21]

Along with these facts, the New Testament also offers substantial instruction designed to make us incurably joyful, victorious people. "Rejoice in the Lord always." "Be joyful always . . . give thanks in all circumstances." Even when persecuted, the apostles found reason to rejoice; even when jailed and shackled, Paul and Silas couldn't stop singing. James's epistle goes as far as telling Christians that their trials should be cause for "pure joy."[22] These passages and many others prove beyond a doubt the obvious but seldom taught truth that *Christians ought to be happy!*

Yet sometimes we hear and think so much about our problems, weaknesses and sufferings that we forget these overwhelming, eternal reasons for celebration. Christians who should be trumpeting victory in Christ are instead bemoaning their own (or, even worse, other people's) sins and shortcomings. Quite likely Paul was addressing just such people when he wrote, "Whatever is right, whatever is pure, whatever is lovely . . . think about such things" (Phil 4:8). Paul did not want his disciples to ignore the negative side of life as if it did not exist—in fact, he had given the Philippians explicit warnings about false teachers just a few verses earlier—but he did want them to devote most of their thinking to the positive side.

Even so, the Bible still displays its heroes in such consuming distress that they could not help talking about it. Jesus in Gethsemane faced depression deeper than any mortal has ever known, and he told his disciples bluntly, "My soul is overwhelmed with sorrow to the point of death" (Mt 26:38). The next day, nailed to a cross, he cried out in desperation that God had forsaken him. Along the same lines, Paul confessed to Timothy his loneliness, his disappointment at his coworkers' desertions and his expectation of imminent death (2 Tim 4:6-16).

Do these examples negate what we have already said about the need for a positive attitude? I think not. Rather, the Bible illustrates that there is such a thing as constructive complaining. The best examples of this are found in those psalms where David dramatically pours out his soul before God.

In Psalm 6 David brings to God an anguished soul, a fear of impending death and an uncontrollable sorrow: "I flood my bed with weeping and drench my couch with tears." He feels as if the answer may never come, but suddenly he knows he has broken through and received the assurance of the Lord's mercy: "The LORD has heard my cry for mercy; the LORD accepts my prayer."

Psalm 13 finds David again feeling hopeless, plagued by the sensation of unanswered prayer. He has had sorrow "every day," his enemies are declaring triumph, and all the while God is hiding his face from him. This time there seems to be no powerful breakthrough, yet David goes away reassured of God's "unfailing love." Despite his woes he can conclude, "I will sing to the LORD, for he has been good to me."

Psalm 22, the most poignant of all David's compositions, embodies a longer, still more difficult struggle for spiritual wholeness. Twice, seeking a remedy for his awful perception that God is silent, David recalls God's faithfulness to him and to his fathers; twice his thoughts return to his present situation and his dismay returns just as quickly. But finally his conviction of ultimate victory is restored, as again he realizes that God "has not despised or disdained the suffering of the afflicted one."

From David's experiences, as recorded in these psalms and many others, we can sketch a checklist of attributes for constructive complaining. First, David went directly to the Lord. He may well have shared his needs with friends also, as Paul did with Timothy, but he concealed nothing from the one who could ultimately change things. Second, unlike some modern teachers, David did not hesitate to "pray the problem"; he described his concerns to God in great detail. Third, he did not glory in his suffering but earnestly prayed for deliverance. Fourth, he persisted until he knew his cry had been heard.[23]

In contrast to David's example, many present-day complainers tell their problems to everyone *except* God. Perhaps they realize that if they went to God, their problems would be taken care of, and they would feel lost if they had nothing to complain about! But we should share our needs with others so that they can become part of the solution. Sometimes they can take action to improve the situation, as did Paul, Peter and John through their epistles when they were alerted to dissension and heresy in the churches. At the very least, they can pray for us. Always, though, we must remember our goal: to become once again the joyful people we are intended to be.

No teacher should be allowed to scare us away from admitting our weaknesses or discouragements; but neither should those weaknesses and discouragements keep us from cultivating the love and joy that are the pre-eminent fruit of the Holy Spirit.

Support or Separate? Criteria for Christian Cooperation

They wasted no time making their presence known on campus. They were on the paths and in front of the main classroom buildings almost daily, handing out leaflets or putting up posters advertising the many activities they had planned for the first few weeks of the term. Free movies and visiting speakers quickly attracted sizable crowds of Christians and other interested inquirers. The leaders seemed young and vivacious. For many it was an exciting experience, one that kept them coming back each week for the remaining years of their college career.

Such was the arrival of Maranatha Campus Ministries at Michigan State University. Maranatha established a branch at that large midwestern campus in fall 1981. I was one of the participants at some of those first meetings, though other church commitments kept me from regular attendance. My contacts with numerous Christian groups enabled me to watch the reaction to Maranatha's presence as, for some campus ministers, initial excitement gave way to bitterness and alarm. Stories began to circulate of students going to Maranatha meetings nightly and failing their classes, or of new Christians dropping all their relationships with friends outside the group.

Similar scenes have occurred at other campuses often' enough to occasion the formation of a committee of six experienced Christian researchers who have examined Maranatha closely and compiled a generally unfavorable report. The issue has produced division within segments of evangelical Christianity.[24] but it has forced all parties to grapple with the uncomfortable possibility that a Christian organization could be fully orthodox in its basic doctrines and yet dangerous in other ways. Christians are realizing that, even though the charismatic and ecumenical movements have sometimes broken down denominational walls and built stronger bonds of unity among believers, it remains necessary to check more than a basic statement of faith before one decides to cooperate with another Christian organization. What criteria are most useful in making that decision? Our analysis of the faith teachings and their effect can help us develop some guidelines.

Since the dangerous extremes of hyper-faith can seldom be spotted by perusing a church's statement of beliefs or by attending a single service, it is necessary to take a close look at the fruits of a given ministry before determining whether we can cooperate with it. Some fruits produced by the faith teachings' most extreme advocates are so rotten that they call for disassociation rather than tolerance. For example, if church members are dying or nearly dying due to the leadership's counsel to refuse medical care, that church is in serious error. The same is the case if sermons on financial prosperity are creating a climate where church members are displaying a self-centered, me-first attitude rather than concentrating first on how they can serve the Lord. Or, if we see sick people being shunned and accused of lack of faith rather than being comforted, we can suspect that bad theology has displaced the love of Christ and cooperation may be impossible.

No matter how serious the problems may be, we owe the churches and individuals preaching such doctrines the kindness and human respect of a direct confrontation. This may demand courage, but it is a necessary step before taking the equally bold step of publicly opposing a ministry that may be sincerely striving to serve God. Several recent incidents within the charismatic movement have demonstrated that leaders can and do change their ways.[25] It is also possible that investigation and confrontation will prove some of the horror stories to be exaggerated rumors. It is always best to check the accuracy of charges before making any public criticisms of individuals, groups or movements. If the charges against a church or a teacher have been substantiated, and if the people involved persist in their views, then at least we will have played our role as watchmen for the truth and will have confidence in the accuracy of our concerns.

Christians outside the faith movement need to realize (as was argued in chapter nine) that not all of the people within the movement are as extreme as the rumors and sporadic tragedies might suggest. Thus, one way in which those outside can create greater unity and reduce the frequency of abuses that discredit Christianity is to encourage their friends on the inside to disassociate themselves from these abuses. Faith pastors have repeatedly expressed their awareness that the movement has spawned some "bad apples."[26] If these pastors will identify the extremes that they repudiate, they will build a basis for agreement with their Christian critics outside the movement and discourage others within the movement from being tempted by the same errors. Very few of us will be able to speak directly with Jerry Savelle or Fred Price, but most of us have friends who have been influenced by faith teachings. So let us all start with those people whom we *can* touch. The process of restoring balance and dismantling the barriers that separate Christians has to begin somewhere.

At the same time, outsiders can build bonds with insiders by stressing areas of agreement. If Charles Farah, one of the strongest critics of the faith message, can still find grounds for shared ministry with Billy Joe Daugherty, pastor of a large faith church in Tulsa, there must remain plenty of room for agreement between the two sides.[27] Individuals can establish relationships with faith adherents by noting those areas where fellowship is definitely possible; churches as a whole can seek opportunities to interact with faith churches and their leaders in evangelistic campaigns, seminars and other activities. Generally speaking, when followers of the faith message are aware of these areas of agreement, they feel more comfortable discussing their beliefs without defensiveness or the fear that they will be perceived as fanatics. Once these bridges have been built, it will be possible to encourage faith Christians to examine critically their methods of Bible study, check carefully the scriptural foundations of their beliefs and achieve a more balanced Christian walk by studying books and topics other than the faith teachers and their specialties.

Of course, the opportunity to heal divisions is available also to those within the movement. Unfortunately, some faith people appear more prone to demand unconditional surrender from their foes than to seek peace. The situation is not improved when one of the movement's major celebrities states, "Faith teachings have been persecuted by carnal-minded believers [who] don't understand what it is to be sons of God."[28] On the other hand, one faith pastor in Pittsburgh has taken the initiative, at his own expense, to hold a monthly luncheon and bring the area's charismatic leaders together in Christian cooperation and unity—proving that self-righteous exclusivism is not a necessary result of the faith message. By developing such bonds faith people will be able to influence positively the remainder of Christianity, helping others find increased faith and power.

Both sides need to abandon the prideful attitude that comes from assuming they have all the right answers. None of us have *all* the right answers; all of us should welcome, not fear, the opportunity to learn from others. Truth will stand in the end. It is time for Christians on both sides to stop writing venomous accusations. And it is time for the faith teachers to seek, rather than avoid, opportunities for dialog with Christian writers and scholars.[29]

Yes, the faith message does incorporate some bad hermeneutics—but who is so perfect as to cast the first stone? Even some of its most vocal critics credit the faith movement with positive achievements. And the argument that groups like the faith movement can only get worse as they get older and larger is not true; in fact, there have been signs that it may be getting better.[30] In this age of barrier-breaking we have seen infant-baptizers work with adult-baptizers, charismatics join with non-charismatics, even Catholics team up with Protestants, all putting aside their differences to strive together toward common goals in the kingdom of God. Let us pray that the same may happen with the faith movement, so that its strengths may energize the whole of Christianity while its shortcomings are repaired.

Appendix on Methodology:
The Perils of a Christian Researcher

Having previously experienced the crossfire of accusations that a book on a contemporary Christian movement can produce, I hope all dialog concerning this book will center on issues of doctrine and practice. For this reason, and so that others may better understand how I reached my conclusions, I want to describe some aspects of my research methodology and some of the attitudes that I brought into this project.

I embarked on this research as a charismatic Christian who had concerns regarding what appeared to be some extreme teachings coming from the faith ministries, particularly in the area of physical healing. I had no reason to doubt the sincerity of Hagin, Copeland and their colleagues, however, and personally believed that the Lord had inspired and used them for his glory as ministers of the gospel.

I decided that the best way to get a systematic exposure to what the faith teachers consider essential truth was to enroll in Kenneth Hagin's Rhema Correspondence Bible School. The course costs $540 and is designed to last three years, covering eighty-three books, booklets and tapes in thirty-two lessons tested by over two thousand true-false questions. The majority of the books used in the course are the Hagin's own writings, though the curriculum also includes books by Gordon Lindsay, John Osteen, Smith Wigglesworth, F. F. Bosworth, representatives of the Assemblies of God and other charismatic or Pentecostal leaders. The course is intended for lay Christians (those interested in full-time ministry are encouraged to come to Tulsa and enroll for two years at Rhema Bible Training Center) and focuses on faith, prayer, healing, the life of Christ, Bible interpretation and central beliefs common to the charismatic movement as a whole.

I enrolled in the correspondence course in October 1984 and completed it in May 1986. Since Rhema would not send books and materials in advance, but only one lesson at a time, this book began to take shape before I had finished the correspondence course. My concerns about developing conclusions based on incomplete evidence were quickly dispelled, however, since the Rhema course turned out to be fairly repetitive in content.

To supplement this course I read the most popular works of other major faith teachers. I also read all the material criticizing the faith movement that I could obtain. Through personal interviews, correspondence and visits to faith churches, I gained as much familiarity with the movement as I could. I did not receive as much assistance as I would have liked from major leaders of the faith movement. Kenneth Hagin sent me a kind letter in which he expressed his regret at strife and division within the Christian community and his decision to abstain from contributing to my work rather than add more fuel to the current controversy. Several other faith pastors and evangelists answered my request for correspondence with encouraging words, but said they were simply too busy to give further help. Most did not answer at all. Nearly all who did respond, though, were mature, discriminating Christians who were willing, even while identifying themselves with the faith movement, to examine it from both sides and suggest possible areas of imbalance. Many of their insights were invaluable in enabling me to go beyond the obvious in my own analysis.

For several reasons, I have attempted to depend almost solely on written materials and avoid using audio tapes as sources for the beliefs of the major faith teachers. First, written materials generally have been prepared with greater care. I have heard a story about one Christian researcher, usually precise in his documentation, who made an inaccurate charge regarding a cult leader in a seminar that was recorded for national distribution by a research organization. Anyone can get carried away in live presentations, and it seems hardly fair to criticize evangelists for comments that they may have made once or twice in taped sermons. Second, the hours of tapes and radio programming to which I have listened have convinced me that these teachers' audio tapes generally repeat what can be found (and analyzed more quickly and less expensively) in books and pamphlets. Third, relying on written materials (as opposed to radio and television programs or private correspondence) should make independent verification of my findings easier. (Researchers wishing to verify a specific point hinging on interviews or private communication, along with any other people who wish to convey questions or comments to this author, are invited to write to me at P.O. Box 14545, Pittsburgh, PA 15234-0545. The confidentiality of contributors to my work may need to be protected in some cases.)

In preparing this book I faced some unavoidable difficulties. Probably the most obvious is one that plagues any investigative study of the charismatic movement: the impossibility of verifying reported experiences. Just a small fraction of Kenneth Hagin's supernatural experiences, if genuine, would require the conclusion that he has lived a very extraordinary life; yet they carry no conclusive signs of fabrication. It can be confidently stated that Pentecostal revivals have wrought many lasting healings and many evanescent ones, but one cannot hope to estimate with any degree of accuracy the relative proportion of successes to failures, let alone reach a statistically reliable judgment whether the evangelists have a significantly better ratio than hypnotists and Christian Scientists. In these and other areas where one's opinion depends more on suspicions and hunches than on reliable data, I have tried to avoid expressing one.

As a Christian I believe there are two principal ways in which the faith teachers or any other Christian ministry can be evaluated: by the fruits in people's lives and according to the truth of Scripture. But it is difficult to measure the fruit of the movement. The faith movement is large and diverse; its countless local branches and forms display varying cases of balance and extremism. Some of the critical material would give the impression that all admirers of Hagin and Copeland are self-centered, ineffective Christians. People within the movement assure us that the cases of hyper-faith are very rare. The truth is somewhere between these two poles, but much more research would be needed to reach a consensus on just where the typical faith church stands. Moreover, specific fruits cannot always be accurately attributed to specific teachers or teachings. If a given church appears mature in doctrine and practice, for example, it may be hard to tell whether it has reached that goal largely through the faith message or through other influences. A Christian who appears self-centered to his friends is not likely to admit this trait in an interview, especially if he knows that his comments will help to form the basis for a critical evaluation of his church. He may not even be aware of his character flaw, and the researcher, not knowing him intimately, will not be able to spot it.

Since both the faith teachers and the majority of their opponents submit to the authority of Scripture, comparing their doctrines with the teachings of the Bible is the most useful method of evaluation. Even here there remain some problems, as hermeneutics, unlike algebra, offers no scientifically verifiable set of right and wrong answers. I am certainly not about to claim absolute reliability for my own Bible interpretation, or for that of any scholar. However, the history of Christian doctrine shows much more continuity than discontinuity, providing grounds for confidence that there does exist a meaningful standard of orthodoxy against which new doctrines can be tested.

Due to these various difficulties, I have based my evaluations predominantly on Scripture; to a lesser extent on personal correspondence, interviews and observation; and very minimally on histories and biographies of the current faith movement and its forerunners.

As a *Christian* researcher, I felt a need to fulfill a spiritual as well as an academic or professional calling. In carrying out this role I have sought to maintain a high level of honesty and integrity, even though I knew that posing as either an admirer of Hagin and Copeland or a severe critic (depending on the situation) might have enabled me to gain more information. I have also sought to avoid the self-righteous condemnation which so often accompanies the conviction that another person's opinions are wrong. To keep myself in line I used the following rule of thumb: If face to face with the person I am criticizing, would I be willing to speak the words I am writing for publication? If not, then those words are not appropriate for publication. This test has, I hope, delivered me from the intemperate bitterness and cheap shots that sometimes slip unnoticed into Christian books.

Abbreviations and Addresses

To aid the reader in locating the sources used in preparing this book, the following list of addresses is provided. Several of the groups listed here are research organizations from which further information, beyond those materials cited in the notes which follow, can be obtained. Abbreviations used in the notes are italicized.

Believer's Voice of Victory (BVV)—see Kenneth Copeland Publications.
CharisLife—Box 12201, Portland, OR 97212.
Christian Answers and Information *(CAI)*—P.O. Box 3295, Chico, CA 95927.
Christian Research Institute *(CRI)*—Box 500, San Juan Capistrano, CA 92693.
Citizens Freedom Foundation *(CFF)*—P.O. Box 608370, Chicago, IL 60626.
Jerry Savelle Ministries—P.O. Box 2228, Fort Worth, TX 76113.
Jimmy Swaggart Ministries—P.O. Box 2250, Baton Rouge, LA 70821-2250.
Kenneth Copeland Publications and *Believer's Voice of Victory* magazine—Fort Worth, TX 76192.
Kenneth Hagin Ministries and *Word of Faith* magazine—P.O. Box 50126, Tulsa, OK 74150.
Kenyon's Gospel Publishing Society—P.O. Box 973, Lynnwood, WA 98036.
Lutheran Church—Missouri Synod, Commission on Organizations *(LC-MS)*—International Center, 1333 South Kirkwood Road, St. Louis, MO 63122-7295.
Presbyterian and Reformed Renewal Ministries—2245 N.W. 39th St., Oklahoma City, OK 73112.
Springs of Living Water Tape Library *(SLW)*—Richardson Springs, CA 95973.
Word of Faith (WF)—see Kenneth Hagin Ministries.

Notes

Chapter 1

[1]Parsons (Kansas) *Sun*, 20-21 March 1982.

[2]Robertson and Oral Roberts are appropriately called "friendly outsiders" to the faith movement in Richard N. Ostling, "Power, Glory—and Politics," *Time*, 17 February 1986, p. 69.

[3]This phrase is a favorite of Kenneth Copeland's and can often be found in his ministry's catalogs or publicity material.

Chapter 2

[1]The award is mentioned in Hobart Freeman, *Positive Thinking and Confession* (Warsaw, Ind.: Faith Publications, n.d.), p. 15.

[2]Jim Quinn and Bill Zlatos, "Freeman Shuns Media, All Publicity," *Fort Wayne News-Sentinel*, 4 May 1983; Douglas Frantz, "Faith No Cure-All, Sect Finds," *Chicago Tribune*, 8 June 1980; John Davis, "Hobart Freeman: Mystic, Monk or Minister?" *Warsaw* (Ind.) *Times-Union*, 27 September 1983. Davis's articles of 27-30 September 1983 are the best source of information on Freeman.

[3]Hobart Freeman, *Charismatic Body Ministry* (Warsaw, Ind.: Faith Publications, n.d.), p. 33; see also pp. 37-39.

[4]John Davis, "Faith Assembly: Haven of Rest or House of Fear?" *Warsaw Times-Union*, 28 September 1983; Quinn and Zlatos, "Freeman Shuns Media."

[5]John Flynn, "Faith Healer's Flock Shuns Needed Care," *Detroit Free Press*, 7 August 1983, on the composition of Faith Assembly; Robert Mapes Anderson, *Vision of the Disinherited* (New York: Oxford Univ. Press, 1983), chaps. 6-7, for the sociological makeup of early Pentecostalism.

[6]Sherman Goldenberg, "Mel Greider: Born-Again People Saver," *Fort Wayne Journal-Gazette,* 19 March 1978.

[7]Davis, "Faith Assembly"; "Glory Barn Founder Dies," *Warsaw Times-Union,* 17 April 1980; Quinn and Zlatos, "Freeman Shuns Media."

[8]Barbara Eagan, "Members of the 'Faith' See Prayer as the Cure-All," *South Bend Tribune,* 1 June 1981.

[9]Eagan, "Members of the 'Faith.' "

[10]Kathy Muckle, "Faith Assembly Followers Banded Together by Fear" and "It Appears To Be a Case of Mind Control," *Warsaw Times-Union,* 27 June 1981; Jim Quinn and Bill Zlatos, "Faith Assembly Rejects Dissent," *Fort Wayne News-Sentinel,* 3 May 1983.

[11]Karl Roebling, *Is There Healing Power?* (Elgin, Ill.: David C. Cook, 1972), p. 79.

[12]John Davis, "Faith Assembly Leader Private, Intense," *Fort Wayne Journal-Gazette,* 13 November 1983; John Davis, "Inspiration for Living or Invitation to Death?" *Warsaw Times-Union,* 29 September 1983.

[13]Flynn, "Faith Healer's Flock"; Dave Surette (father of a former member), letter to author, 28 December 1984.

[14]"A Litany of Death," *Fort Wayne News-Sentinel,* 2 June 1984.

[15]Jim Quinn and Bill Zlatos, "Assembly's Message Ominous," *Fort Wayne News-Sentinel,* 2 June 1984; various *Warsaw Times-Union* articles, November and December 1984.

[16]Quinn and Zlatos, "Assembly's Message Ominous."

[17]A catalog advertising this book as "new" was received by the author from Freeman's ministry in November 1984, just before his death. On the doctrine of spiritual death, see the last footnote to chap. 7.

[18]John Gardner, letter to author, 13 November 1984; Jo Rector, "Freeman: No Headlines for Glory Barn Success," *Warsaw Times-Union,* 12 July 1976; Barbara Eagan, "Faith Assembly: Congregation or Cult?" *South Bend Tribune,* 31 May 1981; "The Faith of Faith Assembly," *Cornerstone,* vol. 12, issue 67 (1983), p. 30.

[19]John Davis, "Faith Assembly: A Look inside the Future," *Warsaw Times-Union,* 30 September 1983; Gardner, letter to author, 13 November 1984.

[20]The quotations are from Freeman, *Positive Thinking,* pp. 19, 7, 33; Hobart Freeman, *Faith for Healing* (Warsaw, Ind.: Faith Publications, n.d.), p. 10; Freeman, *Charismatic Body,* p. 53.

[21]"Atlanta Center Documents High Death Rate in Sect," *Fort Wayne News-Sentinel,* 1 June 1984. For more information related to children's medical care in Faith Assembly and other religious groups, contact CHILD (Children's Healthcare Is a Legal Duty), P.O. Box 2604, Sioux City, IA 51106.

[22]Davis, "Tragedy Often Hits"; personal interviews and correspondence.

[23]Freeman, *Faith,* p. 3; Freeman, *Charismatic Body,* p. 52.

[24]Freeman, *Faith,* p. 13; Freeman, *Positive Thinking,* p. 30; Freeman, *Charismat-*

ic Body, p. 52.

[25]Freeman, *Charismatic Body,* p. 73. It is not clear what Freeman would need to see in the Scriptures as adequate justification for the use of medicine; however, in view of the primitive state of medical science in biblical times, one can hardly imagine a more solid justification than Isaiah 38:21, where the prophet prescribes a distinctly medical cure for the illness of King Hezekiah.

[26]Freeman, *Faith,* p. 4.

[27]Freeman, *Positive Thinking,* p. 54; Quinn and Zlatos, "Assembly's Message Ominous."

[28]Freeman, *Faith,* pp. 26-27; Freeman, *Positive Thinking,* p. 43; personal interview. Former member Teresa Parli reports that "Pray for me, I'm healed in Jesus' name" was a way to communicate health problems surreptitiously at the Faith Assembly branch in West Lafayette, Indiana ("Faith Assembly Members Desire Change in Law," *Fort Wayne News-Sentinel,* 3 May 1983).

[29]Surette, letter to author, 28 December 1984. For a brief, solid examination of recruiting procedures see Robert W. Dellinger, "Cults and Kids: A Study of Coercion" (Boys Town, Neb.: The Boys Town Center, rpt. 1983; available from Citizens Freedom Foundation, Box 266, McFarland, WI 53558).

[30]Charles Farah, Jr., *From the Pinnacle of the Temple* (Plainfield, N.J.: Logos, 1980), pp. 55-56.

[31]Freeman, *Charismatic Body,* p. 69.

[32]Kathy Muckle, "Faith Assembly Mourns Death of Leader," *Warsaw Times-Union,* 10 December 1984. For the events surrounding Freeman's death and subsequent developments in the church see Gary Lewis, "Faith Assembly Followers 'Shackled,' Says Jack Farrell" and "There Have Been Changes within Faith Assembly," *Warsaw Times-Union,* 10 July 1986.

[33]Bill and Beate Almond, letter to the editor, *Cornerstone,* vol. 13, issue 70 (1984), p. 5.

[34]For one of the more respected expressions of this view, see Francis MacNutt, *Healing* (Notre Dame, Ind.: Ave Maria Press, 1974; rpt. New York: Bantam, 1977), pp. 14, 16 (Bantam edition).

[35]"The Faith of Faith Assembly," p. 30.

Chapter 3

[1]"Refreshing Move of God's Spirit Gives Foretaste of Coming Revival," *WF,* May 1983, pp. 4-7; the photographs are on p. 5.

[2]Philip Lochhaas, letter to author, 10 December 1984.

[3]Personal correspondence from a committee member.

[4]Mrs. Oliphant, *The Life of Edward Irving,* vol. 2, 2nd ed. (London: Hurst and Blackett, 1962). The quotations come from pp. 199, 104; see pp. 129-39, 190-221 on the Pentecostal outbreak.

[5]A. J. Gordon, *The Ministry of Healing,* 5th ed. (New York: Revell, 1881), pp.

146-52; William Edward Biederwolf, *Whipping-Post Theology* (Grand Rapids, Mich.: Eerdmans, 1934), pp. 203-4.

[6]A. J. Gordon, *Ministry of Healing*, pp. 158-62; Morton Kelsey, *Healing and Christianity in Ancient Thought and Modern Times* (New York: Harper & Row, 1973), pp. 235-36. Kelsey refers to Barth on pp. 23, 236-37. Arno Gaebelein, an opponent of nearly all that he saw done in the name of faith healing, felt able to approve the work of Trudel and Blumhardt, largely since "nothing of the fanatical of later movements, such as speaking in tongues, occurred." See his book *The Healing Question* (New York: Our Hope, 1925), p. 65.

[7]A. J. Gordon, *Ministry of Healing*, pp. 162-64; Biederwolf, *Whipping-Post*, pp. 170-71.

[8]A. J. Gordon, *Ministry of Healing*, pp. 171-74; Biederwolf, *Whipping-Post*, pp. 207-8; A. W. Tozer, *Wingspread* (Harrisburg, Pa.: Christian Publications, 1943), p. 77. Biederwolf gives Cullis credit for combining medicine with prayer, but Tozer states that Cullis "discontinued the use of other means" and utilized prayer alone.

[9]On Gordon's prominence, see, e.g., Ernest Sandeen, *The Roots of Fundamentalism: British and American Millenarianism 1800-1930* (Chicago: Univ. of Chicago Press, 1970), pp. 142-44, 160-61; George W. Dollar, *A History of Fundamentalism in America* (Greenville, S.C.: Bob Jones University Press, 1973), pp. 19-26. Gordon's son recorded many of his frequent conference appearances in Ernest B. Gordon, *Adoniram Judson Gordon: A Biography*, 2nd ed. (New York: Revell, 1896).

[10]A. J. Gordon, *Ministry of Healing*, p. 16; examples from church history are cited throughout chapters 4-6, 8-9. Readers interested in early church testimonies to healing but without access to Gordon's book are referred to Charles Hummel, *Fire in the Fireplace* (Downers Grove, Ill.: InterVarsity Press, 1978), chap. 17; Keith Bailey, *Divine Healing: The Children's Bread* (Harrisburg, Pa: Christian Publications, 1977), pp. 200-210.

[11]A. J. Gordon, *Ministry of Healing*, pp. 212-14; these issues are discussed further on pp. 198-202, 232-34.

[12]Ernest B. Gordon, *Adoniram Judson Gordon*, pp. 333-35, 369-71. Henry Frost, in *Miraculous Healing* (New York: Revell, 1952), p. 49, inaccurately charges that Gordon's theology ruled out medicine as a justifiable means of healing.

[13]A. J. Gordon, *Ministry of Healing*, p. 221.

[14]A. B. Simpson, *The Gospel of Healing* (Harrisburg, Pa: Christian Publications, 1915), pp. 153-67 (the quotation is on p. 160); Tozer, *Wingspread*, pp. 70-81, 127-28.

[15]Tozer, *Wingspread*, pp. 79-80.

[16]A. B. Simpson, *The Four-Fold Gospel* (Harrisburg, Pa: Christian Publications, 1925), pp. 47-48, 60-62, 64; Simpson, *Gospel of Healing*, pp. 68, 181; Biederwolf, *Whipping-Post*, pp. 184-86.

[17] Simpson, *Gospel of Healing*, pp. 39, 57.

[18] Tozer, *Wingspread*, pp. 138-42.

[19] See especially Simpson, *Gospel of Healing*, p. 182.

[20] The primary available work on Dowie is Gordon Lindsay, *The Life of John Alexander Dowie* (Dallas, Tex.: Voice of Healing, 1951). Kenneth E. Hagin retells the story of Dowie's first healings in *Redeemed from Poverty, Sickness and Death* (Tulsa, Okla.: Kenneth Hagin Ministries, 1983), pp. 17-20.

[21] David Edwin Harrell, *All Things Are Possible* (Bloomington: Indiana Univ. Press, 1975), p. 13.

[22] Anderson, *Vision*, pp. 72, 128-29; "A Berean," *Divine Healing under the Lens* (New York: Charles C. Cook, 1906), pp. 23, 30, 56, 60. Dowie's book entitled *Doctors, Drugs, and Devils* is cited by Rowland V. Bingham, *The Bible and the Body* (London: Marshall, Morgan & Scott, 1921), p. 21; see also Biederwolf, *Whipping-Post*, pp. 195-96.

Tozer (*Wingspread*, pp. 134-35) tells a wonderful story illustrating the difference between Dowie and Simpson. Dowie, who "could see nothing but healing," proposed to Simpson that the two cross the country together preaching healing; Simpson turned him down, and Dowie promptly arranged a series of lectures in which he would preach *against* Simpson. His reputation drew a large crowd in Pittsburgh, the tour's first stop. "That evening, an hour or so before time for the opening lecture, Dowie was eating a fish dinner when a tiny bone became lodged cross-wise in his throat. The crowds waited, time went on and the speaker did not appear. He never showed up. It must have been an eloquent piece of bone, for it completely changed the plans of Mr. Dowie. He cancelled his series of lectures and crept back home to lick his wounds. When Simpson was informed of the turn things had taken, he said simply, 'Oh, Dowie. Yes, I committed that man to God long ago.' "

[23] Anderson, *Vision*, pp. 47-78, which provides as exhaustive a history of Pentecostalism's beginnings as can possibly be researched.

[24] Ibid., pp. 137-52.

[25] On McPherson see Robert Bahr, *Least of All Saints* (Englewood Cliffs, N.J.: Prentice-Hall, 1979), esp. pp. 158-59, 161-62, 291 on healing; Lately Thomas, *Storming Heaven* (New York: Morrow, 1970); Gaebelein, *Healing Question*, pp. 88-89, on her alleged screening procedure.

[26] Stanley Howard Frodsham, *Smith Wigglesworth: Apostle of Faith* (Springfield, Mo.: Gospel Publishing House, 1948; the quotation is from p. 147); Smith Wigglesworth, *Ever Increasing Faith*, rev. ed. (Springfield, Mo.: Gospel Publishing House, 1971).

[27] F. F. Bosworth, *Christ the Healer* (Washington, D.C.: Charles O. Benham, 1924; rpt. Old Tappan, N.J.: Revell, 1973), p. 208.

[28] Harrell, *All Things*, pp. 14-15; Wade H. Boggs, Jr., *Faith Healing and the Christian Faith* (Richmond, Va.: John Knox Press, 1956), pp. 13-14. Bos-

worth's son states in an introduction to the 1973 edition of *Christ the Healer* (p. 5), "I'm sure my father did not realize that the truth [he] received was fifty years ahead of its time" (*Christ the Healer,* pp. 3-4). T. L. Osborn, in *Healing the Sick* (Tulsa, Okla.: Osborn Foundation, 1959), p. 203, says that all Christians should read Bosworth's book; Hagin's praise of Bosworth can be found in *What To Do When Faith Seems Weak and Victory Lost* (Tulsa, Okla.: Kenneth Hagin Ministries, 1979), p. 71, and *The Name of Jesus* (Tulsa, Okla.: Kenneth Hagin Ministries, 1979), p. 10.

[29]T. J. McCrossan, *Bodily Healing and the Atonement* (Youngstown, Ohio: Clement Humbard, 1930; rpt. Tulsa, Okla.: Kenneth Hagin Ministries, 1982).

[30]Biederwolf, *Whipping-Post,* pp. 11-12, 46-47, 90. He quotes one evangelist anonymously as saying, "I never knew what crowds were until I took healing into my program" (p. 11). The speaker is probably Bosworth, who, Biederwolf later writes in a brief biographical sketch, "rose with meteor-like rapidity from the ranks of the more ordinary evangelist engaged in legitimate soul-winning to a position in the healing program" drawing large crowds (pp. 213-14).

[31]"A Berean," *Divine Healing,* pp. 61-62; Oral Roberts, *The Call* (Garden City, N.Y.: Doubleday, 1972), p. 29; David Edwin Harrell, *Oral Roberts: An American Life* (Bloomington: Indiana Univ. Press, 1985), p. 18. Similar stories are recalled in Vinson Synan, *The Holiness-Pentecostal Movement in the United States* (Grand Rapids, Mich.: Eerdmans, 1971), pp. 90-92, 189.

[32]Biederwolf, *Whipping-Post,* pp. 91-92; Gaebelein, *Healing Question,* pp. 95-97.

[33]Harrell, *All Things,* p. 18.

[34]Kenneth E. Hagin, *I Believe in Visions* (Old Tappan, N.J.: Revell, 1972), pp. 9-26.

[35]Ibid., p. 28.

[36]Ibid., pp. 29-30. Hagin says that a doctor confirmed the healing and told him that "people with the type of heart condition that I had almost never get well." Hagin does not specifically identify the disease he had, but he describes its symptoms further in *How You Can Be Led by the Spirit of God* (Tulsa, Okla.: Kenneth Hagin Ministries, 1978), pp. 87-88; Kenneth E. Hagin, *Right and Wrong Thinking* (Tulsa, Okla.: Kenneth Hagin Ministries, 1966), p. 28.

[37]Hagin, *I Believe,* p. 30; Earl Rogers, " 'Long, Lanky Boy' Remembered," *WF,* October 1981, p. 9.

[38]Hagin, *What To Do,* pp. 34, 47; Hagin, *I Believe,* pp. 30-39, 49, 85.

[39]Hagin, *How You Can Be Led,* pp. 47-48, 119-22; Hagin, *I Believe,* pp. 125-26. The quotation is from Rogers, " 'Long, Lanky Boy.' " The world convention of the Full Gospel Business Men's Fellowship International in 1967 included an appearance by Hagin. MacNutt, *Healing,* p. 103, chooses Hagin as his prime example of extreme healing teaching, suggesting that Hagin was certainly a major figure by the early 1970s.

[40]Oral Roberts, *My Story* (Tulsa, Okla.: Summit Book Co., 1961), pp. 2-3, 15-

37; Roberts, *The Call*, pp. 20-35; Harrell, *Oral Roberts*, pp. 3-7, 35-36.

[41]Oral Roberts, *My Twenty Years of a Miracle Ministry* (Tulsa, Okla.: Oral Roberts Evangelistic Association, 1967), p. 7; Roberts, *The Call*, p. 34.

[42]Roberts, *My Story*, pp. 89-97; Roberts, *The Call*, pp. 41-43; Harrell, *Oral Roberts*, pp. 67-69.

[43]Roberts, *My Story*, pp. 130-40, 171; Roberts, *My Twenty Years*, pp. 13-14, 20-23; Harrell, *Oral Roberts*, pp. 81-83, 114-18, 123-30, 177.

[44]Harrell, *All Things*, pp. 146-49; Harrell, *Oral Roberts*, pp. 153-55; Roberts, *The Call*, pp. 129-30.

[45]The material on Kuhlman is based on Jamie Buckingham's authorized biography, *Daughter of Destiny* (Plainfield, N.J.: Logos, 1976).

[46]Buckingham, *Daughter of Destiny*, pp. 100-101.

[47]Subsequent medical verification of several healings obtained at Kuhlman meetings has been provided by physician Richard Casdorph in *The Miracles* (Plainfield, N.J.: Logos, 1976). On the other hand, surgeon William L. Nolen, who visited a Kuhlman miracle service in Minneapolis during his research for *Healing: A Doctor in Search of a Miracle* (New York: Harper & Row, 1974), has taken a very skeptical view of her work.

[48]Buckingham, *Daughter of Destiny*, pp. 117, 122-23, 195.

[49]Bennett tells his story in *Nine O'Clock in the Morning* (Plainfield, N.J.: Logos, 1970). On charismatic renewal in the main-line denominations, see Kilian McDonnell, *Presence, Power, Praise: Documents on the Charismatic Renewal*, 3 vols. (Collegeville, Minn.: Liturgical Press, 1980).

[50]See Bruce Barron, *If You Really Want To Follow Jesus* (Buffalo, N.Y.: Partners, 1981), pp. 7-15; James Connolly, "The Charismatic Movement: 1967-1970," in Kevin and Dorothy Ranaghan, *As the Spirit Leads Us* (New York: Paulist, 1971), pp. 211-32. Of course, the charismatic movement's chances for survival in the Catholic Church would have been much slimmer had not the Second Vatican Council of 1962-1965 already introduced the church to radical, sweeping change.

[51]A. A. Allen, *God's Guarantee to Heal You!* (Miracle Valley, Ariz.: A. A. Allen Publications, 1950), pp. 151-58.

[52]Allen, *God's Guarantee*, pp. 123-25, 141-42; Morris, *The Preachers* (New York: St. Martin's Press, 1973), pp. 23-53; Harrell, *All Things*, pp. 66-75.

[53]Morris, *The Preachers*, p. 51; Harrell, *All Things*, pp. 196-202.

[54]Harrell, *All Things*, pp. 185-86.

[55]See the following issues and page numbers from *WF:* July 1981, pp. 6, 11; October 1981, pp. 10, 12; December 1982, p. 5; October 1983, p. 13; October 1985, p. 17.

[56]Hagin, Jr., notes that "the smart preachers learned from my dad" and names John Osteen, a prolific author and prominent faith teacher from Houston, and Kenneth Copeland as examples. See *Faith Worketh by Love* (Tulsa, Okla.: Kenneth Hagin Ministries, 1983), p. 21.

[57]Gloria Copeland, *God's Will for You* (Ft. Worth, Tex.: Kenneth Copeland Publications, 1972), p. x.

[58]Ibid., p. xii.

[59]Ibid.; Kenneth Copeland, "Believer's Voice of Victory" radio program, 7 May 1985. Charles Farah suggests that the perceived difference in value between Roberts and Hagin was greater than Gloria is willing to state in print: he quotes Kenneth Copeland as saying that he "learned nothing" during six months at Oral Roberts University but was so excited by Hagin's teachings that "he offered the title to his car to purchase Kenneth Hagin tapes" and spent the next month in his garage listening to them. See Farah's article "A Critical Analysis: The 'Roots and Fruits' of Faith-Formula Theology," *Pneuma*, Spring 1981, p. 15.

[60]"Let's Go for It Together!" *BVV*, January 1984, p. 6, for the Copeland ministry statistics. Copeland was rated the fourth most popular male vocalist in one Christian music poll; see *Charisma*, July 1985, p. 63.

[61]"Kenneth Copeland Biography," unpub., obtained from Kenneth Copeland Ministries in February 1985.

[62]Jerry Savelle, *Living in Divine Prosperity* (Tulsa, Okla.: Harrison House, 1982), pp. 37-38; unpublished "résumé" supplied by Jerry Savelle Ministries.

[63]"Campmeeting Report," *WF*, October 1983, pp. 11-12; Stephen Strang, "The Ever Increasing Faith of Fred Price," *Charisma*, May 1985, pp. 20-27.

[64]Osborn, *Healing the Sick*, pp. 204-10; Harrell, *All Things*, pp. 63-65. Morris draws the parallel between Osborn and Roberts in *The Preachers*, pp. 58, 77.

[65]Harrell, *All Things*, pp. 171-72.

[66]Sherry Andrews, "Maranatha Ministries," *Charisma*, May 1982, pp. 20-27; Bob and Rose Weiner, *Bible Studies for a Firm Foundation* (Gainesville, Fla.: Maranatha Publications, 1980), pp. 31-34, 61-64, 77-90.

[67]Stephen Strang, "Robert Tilton Wants You to Be a Success in Life!" *Charisma*, July 1985, pp. 24-27, 79-83.

[68]Simpson, *Four-Fold Gospel*, p. 62.

[69]James 1:5 suggests that the verses which follow it may refer only to prayers for wisdom, not to prayer in general, but this passage is used frequently by positive-confession teachers. See, e.g., Kenneth E. Hagin, *Healing Belongs to Us* (Tulsa, Okla.: Kenneth Hagin Ministries, 1969), pp. 31-32.

[70]Lillian Yeomans, three of whose books are used in the Hagin ministry's correspondence course, was among the first to clearly mix positive confession and healing; see *The Great Physician* (Springfield, Mo.: Gospel Publishing House, rpt. 1976), pp. 30-31. Biographical data on Kenyon appear in Don Gossett and E. W. Kenyon, *The Power of the Positive Confession of God's Word*, enlgd. ed. (Tulsa, Okla.: Custom Graphics, 1981), pp. 208-10. The connection to mind-science teachings has been explored by Dan McConnell in "The Hagin-Kenyon Connection" (Th.M. thesis, Oral Roberts University, 1982). Kenyon's daughter notes that at the time of his death his radio program was

aired only in Seattle and his magazine was little known outside that area (Ruth Kenyon Housworth, letter to author, 16 July 1986); so it is clear that most of his influence has been indirect (through other ministries that have restated many of his ideas) rather than direct.

[71]Similar thoughts can be found throughout Kenyon's work; these specific quotations were taken from his books *The Two Kinds of Faith*, 13th ed. (Lynnwood, Wash.: Kenyon's Gospel Publishing Society, 1969), pp. 66-67, and *Jesus the Healer*, 22nd ed. (Lynnwood, Wash.: Kenyon's Gospel Publishing Society, 1968), pp. 77, 88.

[72]Bosworth cites Kenyon in *Christ the Healer*, p. 148; Osborn does so in *Healing the Sick*, p. 112; Hagin follows suit in his preface to *The Name of Jesus*. McConnell, in "The Hagin-Kenyon Connection," suggests that the parallels between Hagin and Kenyon are so vast and striking as to imply the possibility of extensive borrowing on Hagin's part.

[73]Charles Capps, *The Tongue, a Creative Force* (Tulsa, Okla.: Harrison House, 1976), pp. 63-76, 139. Portions of this book's last two chapters have been published separately as *God's Creative Power Will Work for You* (Tulsa, Okla.: Harrison House, 1976), and the publisher states that 1,120,000 copies of this booklet are in print.

[74]Ruth Kenyon Housworth (letter to author, 8 March 1985) has pointed out that her father poured his money into ministry and died almost penniless.

[75]On Bushnell see Charles C. Cole, *The Social Ideas of the Northern Evangelists 1826-1860* (New York: Octagon, 1966), pp. 169-70; on Conwell see Daniel Bjork, *The Victorian Flight: Russell Conwell and the Crisis of American Individualism* (Washington, D.C.: University Press of America, 1978).

[76]Hagin tells where he believes he received his prosperity doctrine in *How God Taught Me about Prosperity* (Tulsa, Okla.: Kenneth Hagin Ministries, 1985).

[77]Roberts, *My Story*, pp. 87-89, 160-62; Roberts, *My Twenty Years*, p. 23; Harrell, *Oral Roberts*, pp. 65-66, 129-30.

[78]Oral Roberts, *God's Formula for Success and Prosperity* (Tulsa, Okla.: Healing Waters, 1955); Harrell, *All Things*, p. 248, lists Allen's string of publications; Gordon Lindsay, *God's Master Key to Prosperity* (Dallas, Tex.: Christ for the Nations, 1960). Morris, *The Preachers*, p. 31, tells how Allen sold small pieces of his old tent, calling them "Prosperity Blessing Cloths." Harrell (p. 229) says that in the 1960s "Third John 2 became the most quoted text in the revival."

Chapter 4

[1]In describing the movement systematically and at length, I believe I am breaking new ground. Farah's *From the Pinnacle* (see "The Faith Theology," pp. 115-65) contains more critique than explanation of the faith message. Brian Onken, "The Atonement of Christ and the 'Faith' Message," *Forward* 7 (1): pp. 1, 10-15, is an exception, but it deals only with Christ's supposed

spiritual death and rebirth.

[2]Among the good books supportive of charismatic renewal are Hummel, *Fire in the Fireplace*, and George Mallone, *Those Controversial Gifts* (Downers Grove, Ill.: InterVarsity Press, 1983). Among the most influential attacks on Pentecostal-charismatic theology in this century have been B. B. Warfield, *Counterfeit Miracles* (Edinburgh: Banner of Truth Trust, 1918, rpt. 1976); Frederick Dale Bruner, *A Theology of the Holy Spirit: The Pentecostal Experience and the New Testament Witness* (Grand Rapids, Mich.: Eerdmans, 1970); and John MacArthur, *The Charismatics* (Grand Rapids, Mich.: Zondervan, 1978).

[3]If examining the truth claims of Christianity is an issue you want to pursue, some of the best sources are C. S. Lewis, *Mere Christianity* (New York: Macmillan, 1952); Josh McDowell, *Evidence That Demands a Verdict* (San Bernardino, Calif.: Here's Life, 1972); Clark Pinnock, *Reason Enough* (Downers Grove, Ill.: InterVarsity Press, 1980).

[4]Hagin, *Name of Jesus*, p. 30; Kenneth E. Hagin, *New Thresholds of Faith* (Tulsa, Okla.: Kenneth Hagin Ministries, 1972), p. 53; Gloria Copeland, *God's Will for You*, p. 3; Kenyon, *Jesus the Healer*, p. 48. It should be stressed that the notes in this chapter give only a few references for each central doctrinal point and are by no means exhaustive; many of the central statements included in this brief systematic theology could be documented in dozens of sources.

[5]Gloria Copeland, *God's Will for You*, pp. 37-39; Kenneth Copeland, *Welcome to the Family* (Fort Worth, Tex.: Kenneth Copeland Publications, 1979), p. 22; Bosworth, *Christ the Healer*, p. 23; Kenyon, *Jesus the Healer*, pp. 62-63; Kenneth E. Hagin, *Seven Things You Should Know about Divine Healing* (Tulsa, Okla.: Kenneth Hagin Ministries, 1979), pp. 17-21.

[6]Kenneth E. Hagin, *Three Big Words* (Tulsa, Okla.: Kenneth Hagin Ministries, 1983), pp. 1-6; Kenneth Copeland, *The Laws of Prosperity* (Fort Worth, Tex.: Kenneth Copeland Publications, 1974), p. 49.

[7]Hagin, *Name of Jesus*, pp. 29-32; Kenneth E. Hagin, *The Present Day Ministry of Jesus Christ* (Tulsa, Okla.: Kenneth Hagin Ministries, 1983), pp. 6-8; Gloria Copeland, *God's Will for You*, p. 5; Kenneth E. Hagin, *El Shaddai* (Tulsa, Okla.: Kenneth Hagin Ministries, 1980), p. 7; E. W. Kenyon, *What Happened from the Cross to the Throne* (Lynnwood, Wash.: Kenyon's Gospel Publishing Society, 1966); Kenneth Copeland, cassette, "What Happened from the Cross to the Throne" (Fort Worth, Tex.: Kenneth Copeland Publications, n.d.).

[8]Kenneth Copeland, *Welcome*, pp. 21-22; Hagin, *Redeemed*, pp. 5, 15; Kenneth Hagin, Jr., *Get Acquainted with God* (Tulsa, Okla.: Kenneth Hagin Ministries, 1983), pp. 11-12; Charles Capps, *Releasing the Ability of God through Prayer* (Tulsa, Okla.: Harrison House, 1978), p. 123.

[9]Joe Magliato, *The Wall Street Gospel* (Eugene, Oreg.: Harvest House, 1981), pp. 51-52; Shirley Finkenbinder Holloway, "What's Wrong with the Positive

Confession Teachings?" *Pentecostal Evangel,* 10 July 1983, p. 9.

[10]Kenneth Hagin, Jr., "The Devil and His Kingdom," *WF,* June 1984, p. 2. In defense of Magliato and Holloway, it must be said that I cannot find this distinction between the curse of the law and the curse of the Fall in any earlier faith materials, and that it may have been developed later in response to this criticism.

[11]Hagin, *New Thresholds,* pp. 46, 53; Kenneth Copeland, *Laws of Prosperity,* pp. 51-54.

[12]Kenneth E. Hagin, *Prevailing Prayer to Peace* (Tulsa, Okla.: Kenneth Hagin Ministries, 1973), pp. 11-12; E. W. Kenyon, *The Two Kinds of Knowledge* (Lynnwood, Wash.: Kenyon's Gospel Publishing Society, 1966); Kenneth E. Hagin, *The Real Faith* (Tulsa, Okla.: Kenneth Hagin Ministries, 1970), p. 5.

[13]Hagin, *Seven Things,* pp. 7-8; Hagin, *Name of Jesus,* pp. 122-23; Bosworth, *Christ the Healer,* pp. 24-25.

[14]Hagin, *What To Do,* p. 96; Hagin, *Healing Belongs to Us,* p. 11; Gordon Lindsay, *The Life and Teachings of Christ,* 3 vols. (Dallas, Tex.: Christ for the Nations, rpt. 1982), I:159-60. Lindsay's three-volume series remains worthy of inclusion as an important example of faith theology; it is among the first books assigned in Hagin's correspondence course.

[15]Kenyon, *Jesus the Healer,* p. 67; Hagin, *Redeemed,* p. 20.

[16]Gloria Copeland, *God's Will for You,* p. 73; Bosworth, *Christ the Healer,* p. 50.

[17]Gloria Copeland, *God's Will for You,* pp. 57-60; Bosworth, *Christ the Healer,* pp. 190-206.

[18]Hagin, *What To Do,* p. 96; Hagin, *Seven Things,* pp. 13-15; Capps, *Releasing the Ability,* p. 68; Gloria Copeland, *God's Will for You,* p. 84; Lindsay, *Life and Teachings,* I:163-64.

[19]John Osteen, *This Awakening Generation* (Houston, Tex.: John Osteen Publications, 1978), pp. 47, 86; Gloria Copeland, *God's Will for You,* p. 73.

[20]Lindsay, *Life and Teachings,* I:209, III:28; Gloria Copeland, *God's Will for You,* pp. 52, 85; Hagin, *Seven Things,* p. 65.

[21]Kenneth E. Hagin, *Exceedingly Growing Faith* (Tulsa, Okla.: Kenneth Hagin Ministries, 1983), pp. 10-11; Hagin, *Seven Things,* pp. 7, 14; Bosworth, *Christ the Healer,* pp. 7, 80-92.

[22]Walter Martin, cassette, "The Errors of Positive Confession" (San Juan Capistrano, Calif.: Christian Research Institute, n.d.).

[23]Hagin, *El Shaddai,* pp. 21-24; Hagin, *Seven Things,* p. 21; Kenyon, *Jesus the Healer,* p. 65; Bosworth, *Christ the Healer,* p. 41. Hagin refers to the deaths of Bosworth and Kenyon in the preface to *The Name of Jesus.* Kenyon's daughter has basically substantiated the claim for her father, stating that he felt tired one morning, slipped into a coma around 9 A.M., and was dead by noon (Ruth Kenyon Housworth, letter to author, 8 March 1985).

[24]Kenneth E. Hagin, *The Believer's Authority* (Tulsa, Okla.: Kenneth Hagin Ministries, 1983), p. 36; Lindsay, *Life and Teachings,* I:202; Hagin, *What To*

Do, pp. 77-79.

[25]Hagin, *Seven Things,* p. 59; Gloria Copeland, *God's Will for You,* p. 76.

[26]Kenyon, *Jesus the Healer,* p. 18; Hagin, *Real Faith,* pp. 17-18; Gloria Copeland, *God's Will for You,* pp. 47, 55; Osborn, *Healing the Sick,* pp. 17-20.

[27]Bosworth, *Christ the Healer,* pp. 163-75, discusses the congregation's lack of faith among causes of failure. Current faith teachers seldom speak of congregational responsibility if a healing does not occur, though they do speak of the individual's unbelief as a factor.

[28]Hagin, *Present Day Ministry,* p. 22; Hagin, *New Thresholds,* p. 39; Hagin, *Prevailing Prayer,* p. 63.

[29]Hagin, *What To Do,* p. 49.

[30]Hagin, *Seven Things,* pp. 37-55. I have heard Hagin refer to the Law of Contact and Transmission in several recordings of healing services, available from *SLW.* See also Kenyon, *Jesus the Healer,* pp. 36-38.

[31]Hagin, *Seven Things,* p. 54; Hagin, *Name of Jesus,* p. 133; Gloria Copeland, *God's Will for You,* p. 82; Kenneth Copeland, *Welcome,* p. 25.

[32]Gloria Copeland, *God's Will Is Prosperity* (Fort Worth, Tex.: Kenneth Copeland Publications, 1978), p. 29; Fred Price, *Faith, Foolishness, or Presumption?* (Tulsa, Okla.: Harrison House, 1979), pp. 64-68, 84-90.

[33]Hagin, *Seven Things,* pp. 63-64; Lindsay, *Life and Teachings,* III:70; Kenneth Copeland, *The Force of Faith* (Fort Worth, Tex.: Kenneth Copeland Publications, 1983), p. 30; Price, *Faith, Foolishness,* p. 83.

[34]Bosworth, *Christ the Healer,* pp. 108, 137; Kenneth Copeland, *Force of Faith,* p. 31; Hagin, *New Thresholds,* p. 9; Capps, *Releasing the Ability,* pp. 115-16.

[35]Kenneth Copeland, *Force of Faith,* p. 10; Hagin, *Exceedingly,* pp. 15-17, 49.

[36]Kenneth E. Hagin, *The Bible Way to Receive the Holy Spirit* (Tulsa, Okla.: Kenneth Hagin Ministries, 1981), p. 13; Hagin, *Prevailing Prayer,* pp. 15, 67; Kenyon, *Jesus the Healer,* p. 20.

[37]Kenneth E. Hagin, *Ministering to the Oppressed* (Tulsa, Okla.: Kenneth Hagin Ministries, 1983), p. 9; Hagin, *New Thresholds,* pp. 10, 24; Hagin, *Exceedingly,* p. 20; Fred Price, *How Faith Works* (Tulsa, Okla.: Harrison House, 1976), p. 62.

[38]Hagin, *Believer's Authority,* p. 63; Lindsay, *Life and Teachings,* I:218, 230; Hagin, *Real Faith,* pp. 6-7.

[39]Hagin, *New Thresholds,* p. 48; Gloria Copeland, *God's Will Is Prosperity,* pp. 71-72.

[40]Kenneth E. Hagin, *In Him* (Tulsa, Okla.: Kenneth Hagin Ministries, 1975), p. 40; Hagin, *Exceedingly,* pp. 13, 101-2; Hagin, *Right and Wrong Thinking,* p. 22; Price, *How Faith Works,* p. 118; Capps, *Releasing the Ability,* p. 38.

[41]Hagin, *What To Do,* p. 108; Hagin, *Name of Jesus,* pp. 135-37; Bosworth, *Christ the Healer,* pp. 140-41; Kenneth Copeland, *Laws of Prosperity,* p. 98.

[42]Hagin, *New Thresholds,* pp. 82-85, finds these four steps in 1 Samuel 17 (David and Goliath), Luke 15 (the prodigal son), and Mark 5:25-34. See also Hagin,

Exceedingly, pp. 75-93. Hagin, *Prevailing Prayer*, pp. 10-15, has a list of seven steps that overlaps this list of four steps.

[43]Bosworth, *Christ the Healer*, p. 8; Hagin, *What To Do*, pp. 100-102.

[44]The faith teachers stress this point incessantly. See, e.g., Kenyon, *The Two Kinds of Faith;* Hagin, *New Thresholds*, pp. 11-13, 74; Hagin, *Real Faith*, pp. 18-20, 24-25; Gloria Copeland, *God's Will Is Prosperity*, pp. 67-68.

[45]Hagin, *Name of Jesus*, p. 141; Hagin, *What To Do*, pp. 97-113; Price, *How Faith Works*, p. 121; Capps, *Releasing the Ability*, p. 40. Hagin takes a softer position on repeated prayer in *Exceedingly*, p. 51.

[46]Kenneth E. Hagin, *The Art of Intercession* (Tulsa, Okla.: Kenneth Hagin Ministries, 1980), pp. 101, 118, 139; Hagin, *What To Do*, pp. 89-90; Capps, *Releasing the Ability*, pp. 25, 36-37.

[47]Hagin, *Prevailing Prayer*, p. 48; Hagin, *What To Do*, p. 90. Jesus' "if it be thy will" prayer in the garden of Gethsemane is explained in this way.

[48]Hagin, *Name of Jesus*, pp. 133, 138-39; Hagin, *What To Do*, pp. 69-71; Hagin, *Right and Wrong Thinking*, pp. 20-21, 31; Capps, *Releasing the Ability*, pp. 93, 107.

[49]Hagin, *New Thresholds*, pp. 86-87, 90-91; Lindsay, *Life and Teachings*, I:230; Hagin, *What To Do*, p. 60; Hagin, *Real Faith*, p. 26; Hagin, *Healing Belongs to Us*, p. 28; Capps, *Releasing the Ability*, pp. 108, 115-17.

[50]Hagin, Jr., *Faith Worketh by Love*. The phrase in the title comes from Galatians 5:6. See also Kenneth Copeland, *Laws of Prosperity*, pp. 110-17.

[51]Kenneth Copeland, *Force of Faith*, pp. 18-19; Gloria Copeland, *God's Will Is Prosperity*, pp. 66-67; Hagin, *Name of Jesus*, p. 76.

[52]Hagin, *What To Do*, pp. 44, 79; Kenneth Hagin, Jr., *Key to the Supernatural* (Tulsa, Okla.: Kenneth Hagin Ministries, 1982), pp. 21-22.

[53]Hagin, *What To Do*, pp. 25-36; Hagin, *Prevailing Prayer*, p. 81; Gloria Copeland, *God's Will for You*, pp. 12, 53.

[54]Hagin, *New Thresholds*, pp. 53-54, 85; Gloria Copeland, *God's Will for You*, p. 27; Kenneth Copeland, *Laws of Prosperity*, pp. 24-25. The common references are to Joshua 1:8 and 3 John 2.

[55]Savelle, *Living in Divine Prosperity*, pp. 53-57; Gloria Copeland, *God's Will Is Prosperity*, pp. 17-23, 37, 41.

[56]Gloria Copeland, *God's Will Is Prosperity*, pp. 47-53; Kenneth Copeland, *Laws of Prosperity*, pp. 66-67, 73, 77-96.

[57]Gloria Copeland, *God's Will Is Prosperity*, p. 45; Kenneth Copeland, *Laws of Prosperity*, p. 107.

[58]Hagin, Jr., *Three Big Words*, p. 12; Hagin, *Believer's Authority*, pp. 16, 40-41; Price, *Faith, Foolishness*, p. 28.

[59]Hagin, Jr., *Faith Worketh by Love*, p. 3; Hagin, *Prevailing Prayer*, pp. 52-53, and *Praying to Get Results* (Tulsa, Okla.: Kenneth Hagin Ministries, 1983), pp. 11-14, both citing Paul and Silas in Acts 16.

[60]Gloria Copeland, *God's Will for You*, pp. 19-20; Hagin, *Bible Way*, p. 29.

[61]Kenneth Copeland, *Welcome*, p. 20; Hagin, *Bible Way*, pp. 7-9; Gloria Copeland, *God's Will for You*, p. 20, adds several suggestions to this requirement.
[62]Hagin, *Bible Way*, pp. 10-12.
[63]Hagin, Jr., *Faith Worketh by Love*, p. 2.

Chapter 5
[1]Hagin, *Seven Things*, p. 8.
[2]Martin, "Errors of Positive Confession"; Gordon Fee, *The Disease of the Health and Wealth Gospels* (Costa Mesa, Calif.: The Word for Today, 1979; now available from *CRI*), pp. 15-16; Biederwolf, *Whipping-Post*, pp. 288-305.
[3]Bailey, *Divine Healing*, pp. 43-59. The citation of Delitzsch is from his *Biblical Commentary on the Prophecies of Isaiah*, vol. 2 (Edinburgh: T. & T. Clark, 1892), pp. 291-92.
[4]Bailey, *Divine Healing*, pp. 55-57; Mallone, *Those Controversial Gifts*, pp. 105-6; Warfield, *Counterfeit Miracles*, pp. 175-77.
[5]For a more complete discussion of the already and the not yet, and for references to more technical material on the topic, see Joni Eareckson, *A Step Further* (Grand Rapids, Mich.: Zondervan, 1978), pp. 129-34 and n. 10.
[6]Boggs, *Faith Healing*, p. 116.
[7]Robert H. Culpepper, *Evaluating the Charismatic Movement* (Valley Forge, Pa.: Judson, 1977), p. 122. I strongly recommend that both charismatics and noncharismatics read Culpepper's balanced, wonderfully constructive work.
[8]Eareckson, *A Step Further*, pp. 153-58. Frank Bateman Stanger, the late Methodist seminary president who had considerable experience in healing ministry, shares my view in *God's Healing Community* (Nashville, Tenn.: Abingdon, 1978), pp. 69, 109. In defense of Tada, it should be noted that she, unlike many evangelists, is seeking to provide much-needed Christian compassion to the disabled. As she has stated, "I believe God miraculously heals. But I have met thousands of people who are severely disabled, and the number of those who have been miraculously delivered—while they are there—is small by comparison" ("Joy in Caring" seminar, Wheeling, W.Va., 26 April 1986).
[9]Other examples include Mt 8:13; 9:29; 15:28; Mk 10:52; and Lk 5:20; see esp. Mk 5:30 and Lk 8:46 on Jesus' latent power.
[10]Lindsey Pherigo, *The Great Physician* (New York: United Methodist Church, 1983), pp. 21-28.
[11]Gloria Copeland, *God's Will for You*, p. 56; see also Hagin, *Art of Intercession*, p. 27; Kenneth E. Hagin, *The Ministry of a Prophet* (Tulsa, Okla.: Kenneth Hagin Ministries, 1968), p. 5.
[12]Norvel Hayes, *God's Power through Laying On of Hands* (Tulsa, Okla.: Harrison House, 1982), p. 8.
[13]Gloria Copeland, *God's Will for You*, p. 57; Osborn, *Healing the Sick*, pp. 169-73; Gordon Lindsay, *Why Do the Righteous Suffer?* (Dallas, Tex.: Christ for the

Nations, rpt. 1983), pp. 5-12; Bosworth, *Christ the Healer*, pp. 190-206. Their view of Paul's thorn is supported by R. V. G. Tasker, a respected scholar and not a faith teacher, in *The Second Epistle of Paul to the Corinthians* (Grand Rapids, Mich.: Eerdmans, 1958), pp. 173-77.

[14]Hagin, *Seven Things*, pp. 17-20; Hagin, *Ministry of a Prophet*, p. 4; for criticism of this view, Magliato, *Wall Street Gospel*, p. 97.

[15]Osborn (*Healing the Sick*, pp. 173-74) argues that the word used in Gal 4:13 always means "human weakness," not "sickness," but, if his view were correct, it would imply that Jesus took away only our "human weaknesses" in Mt 8:17, where the same word is used. Others within the faith movement have pointed out to me that, since Paul and Timothy were imperfect men, their faith was imperfect too, and thus their sicknesses prove nothing about the availability of healing by faith. However, the Bible does not tell us that these sicknesses were due to weakness of faith, so such a view must be considered speculative. Besides, Paul was clearly a man of great faith, so if perfect health was out of his reach, it would seem presumptuous for any of us to claim it confidently for ourselves.

[16]Magliato, *Wall Street Gospel*, pp. 126-33.

[17]Hagin, *Healing: God at Work* (Tulsa, Okla.: Kenneth Hagin Ministries, n.d.), p. 11, states (on the basis of Job 3:25, and despite Job 1:1, 8) that "Job himself opened the door to the devil by being afraid." See also Lindsay, *Why Do the Righteous Suffer?* pp. 41-44. Hagin, though, deals more wisely with Job in *Redeemed*, p. 9, stating simply that his faith was rewarded and his trial lasted only nine to eighteen months.

[18]Kenneth Hagin, "How to Walk in Love," *WF*, June 1983, pp. 3-4.

[19]Kenneth Hagin, Jr., "Exercising Possibility Faith," *WF*, February 1979, p. 4; Gloria Copeland, *God's Will Is Prosperity*, p. 29.

[20]Price, *Faith, Foolishness*, pp. 64-68, 84-87, 94.

[21]Ibid., p. 90.

[22]See the references in chap. 4, n. 33, and Price, *How Faith Works*, pp. 127-28. Interestingly, even Oral Roberts's famed 1935 healing of tuberculosis was not instantly completed: "The morning after his healing, Oral was back on his mattress, weak and wondering" (Harrell, *Oral Roberts*, p. 35).

[23]There are three passages to which the faith teachers usually appeal as gradual healings by Jesus. John 4:52 (KJV) says that a boy whose father sought Jesus' prayers "began to amend," but the Greek carries no sense of gradual recovery. The ten lepers of whom it is said, "As they went, they were cleansed" (Lk 17:11-14), and the blind man who washed twice before regaining his complete sight (Mk 8:22-26), are both cases of only momentary delays—hardly parallel to the modern cases where people wait days or months after prayer and wonder if healing is still coming.

[24]Biederwolf, *Whipping-Post*, pp. 36-53; James Buckley, *Faith-Healing, Christian Science, and Kindred Phenomena* (New York: Century, 1900), pp. 39-41; Boggs,

Faith Healing, pp. 29-35; John R. Rice, *The Charismatic Movement* (Murfreesboro, Tenn.: Sword of the Lord, 1976), pp. 251-57. Today's faith healers, if they sincerely believe their works match those of Jesus, would do well to submit a handful of immediate healings of medically incurable disorders (e.g., deaf-mutes or total blindness) for independent, public, medical verification; otherwise, it will remain difficult to disprove Buckley and Warfield's claims that Christian faith healers can do only as much as, and no more than, Christian Science, hypnotists and other mind-cure approaches. Buckley, *Faith Healing,* pp. 15-19; Warfield, *Counterfeit Miracles,* p. 191.

[25]Bailey, *Divine Healing,* pp. 27-45.

[26]Ronald A. Ward, "James," in Donald Guthrie, Alec Motyer, Alan M. Stibbs and Donald J. Wiseman, *The New Bible Commentary: Revised* (Grand Rapids, Mich.: Eerdmans, 1970), p. 1235.

[27]Peter H. Davids, *The Epistle of James* (Grand Rapids, Mich.: Eerdmans, 1982), p. 194.

Chapter 6

[1]Fee, *Disease,* p. 9.

[2]Gloria Copeland, *God's Will Is Prosperity,* pp. 48-52.

[3]Kenneth Copeland, *Laws of Prosperity,* pp. 67, 87.

[4]Some of them recognize this requirement, though; see Lindsay, *God's Master Key,* p. 48; Savelle, *Living in Divine Prosperity,* p. 146.

[5]Hagin, *Redeemed,* p. 5. See also Gloria Copeland, *God's Will for You,* pp. 36-37, 40; Savelle, *Living in Divine Prosperity,* p. 126; Kenneth Copeland, *Laws of Prosperity,* pp. 47-50.

[6]Gloria Copeland, *God's Will Is Prosperity,* pp. 38-39; Capps, *The Tongue,* pp. 98, 153.

[7]See Magliato, *Wall Street Gospel,* pp. 51-61.

[8]See, e.g., Gloria Copeland, *God's Will for You,* p. 27; Kenneth Copeland, *Laws of Prosperity,* pp. 13, 51; a series of articles in *BVV,* April 1982-April 1983, which use this verse as an epigraph.

[9]E.g., Kenneth Kantzer, "The Cut-Rate Grace of a Health and Wealth Gospel," *Christianity Today,* 28 June 1985, p. 14.

[10]Fee, *Disease,* p. 4, citing A. S. Hunt and C. C. Edgar, eds., *Select Papyri* (New York: Putnam, 1932), pp. 269-395.

[11]I recognize that some may insist that a promise given to God's people under the old covenant automatically applies to God's people under the new and better (according to Heb 8:6) covenant. Space does not permit me to deal in any detail with the problems of Old Testament interpretation, but the absurdity of this argument can be quickly shown by recalling the often brutal military conquests achieved, with God's blessing, by ancient Israel. Those who wish to apply all Old Testament promises to today ought to be gathering armed bands of Christians and forcibly capturing the best land

they can find. One must be careful to distinguish those promises which were intended for a specific situation from those which have more general application.

[12]Kenneth Copeland, *Laws of Prosperity*, pp. 23, 25; Savelle, *Living In Divine Prosperity*, p. 77.

[13]Kenneth Copeland, "I've Received My Instructions. Our Calling Is Made Clear," *BVV*, January 1985, pp. 2-3.

[14]Kenneth Hagin, Jr., "The Exaltation of Christ," *WF*, April 1985, p. 4. This statement preceded the publication in minibook form, later in 1985, of *How God Taught Me about Prosperity*.

[15]A former Rhema Bible Training Center student reports having heard Hagin make this statement, which as far as I know is not in print.

[16]Charles Hodge, *An Exposition of the Second Epistle to the Corinthians* (New York: Robert Carter and Bros., 1860), p. 220.

[17]C. K. Barrett, *A Commentary on the Second Epistle to the Corinthians* (New York: Harper & Row, 1973), p. 239; Gordon Fee, letter to author, 25 June 1985.

[18]Gloria Copeland, *God's Will Is Prosperity*, p. 45; Kenneth Copeland, *Laws of Prosperity*, pp. 77-84, 29, 37.

[19]Jerry Savelle, *Giving: The Essence of Living* (Tulsa, Okla.: Harrison House, 1982), pp. 22, 72-73.

[20]Richard Lovelace, "Countering the Devil's Tactics," *Charisma*, December 1984, p. 10. Lovelace had expressed his concerns to the author in a letter of 7 April 1983.

[21]Fee is a partial exception here, in that he does recognize some of Copeland's good points before opening his criticisms; see *Disease*, p. 2.

[22]Gloria Copeland, *God's Will Is Prosperity*, p. 20.

[23]These statements by Hagin, Jr., can be found in "Victory Words for Front-Line Battles," *WF*, November 1980, p. 7; *Itching Ears* (Tulsa, Okla.: Kenneth Hagin Ministries, 1982); *Get Acquainted*, pp. 14-16; "Qualifications for the Inheritance," *WF*, January 1984, p. 5.

[24]Savelle, *Living in Divine Prosperity*, pp. 27, 47, 91-92, 178-79, 190.

[25]Magliato, *Wall Street Gospel*, pp. 20-21; Fee, *Disease*, p. 11, makes a similar comment, as do Stanley C. Baldwin, "The Prosperity Fallacy," *Eternity*, October 1979, pp. 46-47, and Jimmy Swaggart, *The Balanced Faith Life* (Baton Rouge, La.: Jimmy Swaggart Ministries, 1981), p. 37.

[26]Farah, *From the Pinnacle*, p. 154.

[27]Kenneth Copeland, "From the Philippines . . . with Love," *BVV*, May-June 1981. Copeland took a similarly reserved view of prosperity when preaching in Zimbabwe in April 1986 (Vinson Synan, interview with author, 22 May 1986).

[28]See esp. Barton Green, "A Winter Harvest," *BVV*, July 1985, pp. 4-5.

[29]Philip Lochhaas, letter to author, 10 December 1984.

[30]Gloria Copeland, *God's Will Is Prosperity*, p. 20.

[31]See Gloria Copeland, *God's Will Is Prosperity,* pp. 2, 5, 7, 10, 11, etc., and Kenneth Copeland, *Laws of Prosperity,* and Savelle, *Living in Divine Prosperity,* passim. Even the Copeland's relatively balanced definition of prosperity has faced criticism. The Assemblies of God, in an official denominational statement, have charged that behind this intention to "use God's ability and power" lies a mindset according to which man, not God, is in control. "This puts man in the position of using God," the document states, "rather than man surrendering himself to be used of God" (*The Believer and Positive Confession* [Springfield, Mo.: Gospel Publishing House, 1980], p. 17).

[32]Savelle, in one extended discussion of 1 Tim 6 (*Living in Divine Prosperity,* pp. 203-7), starts at verse 9, and nowhere in the book does he mention verse 5.

[33]Loren Cunningham, cassette, "God and Finances," available from Youth with a Mission, P.O. Box YWAM, Kailua-Kona, HI 96745-9099.

Chapter 7

[1]Capps, *Releasing the Ability,* pp. 6-7.

[2]Ibid., pp. 79-83.

[3]Ibid., p. 81.

[4]Fee, *Disease,* pp. 16-17.

[5]Capps, *The Tongue,* p. 24; Hagin, *Exceedingly,* p. 10.

[6]Hagin, *What To Do,* pp. 32-33.

[7]Price, *Faith, Foolishness,* pp. 111, 123.

[8]Larry Bishop, "Prosperity," *Cornerstone,* May-June 1981.

[9]Hagin, *Exceedingly,* p. 76.

[10]Capps, *The Tongue,* pp. 151-59.

[11]See esp. Hagin's books *How You Can Know the Will of God* and *How You Can Be Led by the Spirit of God.*

[12]The theological problems in Cho's work have been explored extensively by Bruce DilLavou in "The Problems of Confession," *CAI Newsletter,* Summer 1983, pp. 6-11; Dave Hunt and T. A. McMahon, *The Seduction of Christianity* (Eugene, Oreg.: Harvest House, 1985), pp. 20, 33, 111-14, 139-40, 143-45.

[13]Paul Yonggi Cho, *The Fourth Dimension* (Plainfield, N.J.: Logos, 1979), pp. 97-113.

[14]Hagin, *Prevailing Prayer,* p. 48; Hagin, *Act of Intercession,* p. 6; Hagin, *Exceedingly,* pp. 10-11.

[15]Kenneth Copeland, "Rise and Be Healed," *BVV,* November 1981, p. 3; Gloria Copeland, *God's Will for You,* p. 74.

[16]See Brian Onken, "The Misunderstanding of Faith," *Forward,* February 1983, pp. 5-6, available from CRI.

[17]Magliato, *Wall Street Gospel,* p. 118. The story from Daniel has an interesting parallel in 2 Tim 4:18 where Paul predicts his impending death yet says, "The Lord will rescue me from every evil attack and will bring me safely to

his heavenly kingdom." This passage and Daniel 3 suggest that the Bible sees rescue as spiritual, not necessarily physical, protection.

[18]Gloria Copeland, *God's Will Is Prosperity*, p. 110.

[19]Kenneth Hagin, Jr., "Don't Quit; Your Faith Will See You Through," *WF*, May 1981, p. 4.

[20]Hagin, *Seven Things*, p. 37.

[21]Ibid., p. 42.

[22]Capps, *The Tongue*, p. 39; see also Price, *How Faith Works*, p. 23.

[23]Lillian B. Yeomans, who tried Christian Science unsuccessfully before receiving divine healing from drug addiction and entering her own ministry of healing, convincingly shows the differences between the two belief systems (using direct quotations from Eddy) in *Healing from Heaven* (1926; rev. ed., Springfield, Mo.: Gospel Publishing House, 1973), pp. 85-95.

[24]Hagin, Jr., *Itching Ears*, p. 27.

[25]Hagin, *What To Do*, pp. 99-101.

[26]Ibid., p. 101. Hagin does offer one defense that is somewhat more sophisticated: in Romans 4:17 Abraham is called " 'a father of many nations'— in the presence of God in whom he believed." The Greek word for "in the presence of" is rendered as "like unto" by a King James Version marginal reading. Based on this translation, Hagin argues that Abraham "did just like God did. He called those things which be not as though they were—and that was his faith." Modern translations and Greek scholarship, however, suggest that Hagin has chosen a doubtful rendering. None of the four modern translations I have checked support Hagin's opinion, nor does Thayer's *Greek-English Lexicon of the New Testament* (Grand Rapids, Mich.: Zondervan, 1979), p. 338.

[27]Capps, *The Tongue*, p. 7; this statement draws ire from DilLavou, "Problems of Confession," p. 8.

[28]Capps, *The Tongue*, pp. 12 (also 31), 91, 104; Capps, *Releasing the Ability*, p. 92; compare this last statement to Mt 21:28-31, where Jesus implies that people can say one thing and do another.

[29]Capps, *Releasing the Ability*, pp. 101-2.

[30]Rom 5:8, 2 Cor 5:19, Tit 3:5.

[31]Gal 2:21, Rom 12:6, Heb 4:16. For biblical teaching on grace and humility from within the faith movement, see Kenneth Hagin, Jr., *Blueprint for Building Strong Faith* (Tulsa, Okla.: Kenneth Hagin Ministries, 1980), pp. 20-25.

[32]Jimmy Swaggart accuses the faith movement of "an air of superiority" in *Hyper-Faith: A New Gnosticism?* (Baton Rouge, La.: Jimmy Swaggart Ministries, 1982), p. 18. While most of Swaggart's criticisms do not apply to the whole faith movement, many are accurate assessments of its more extreme portion. For discussion of the opposing danger of guilt, see chaps. 1 and 5.

[33]On the dangers inherent in the themes of "spiritual law" and "you are gods," see Hunt and McMahon, *Seduction of Christianity*, pp. 20-26, 82-88, 97-

98, 101, 106, 147-48. Unfortunately, some misunderstanding of this book's intent and some sensational language on Hunt and McMahon's part have made the book more divisive than it ought to have been. On this point, though, its warnings are important.

³⁴I have chosen not to discuss one issue—the teaching that Jesus "died spiritually" and went to hell to suffer for three days before his resurrection. Kenyon taught this doctrine, and Hagin and Copeland apparently adopted it from him. Critics charge that it ignores Jesus' words on the cross, "It is finished," and devalues his sacrificial death by suggesting that the crucifixion was not sufficient to redeem us from sin. Some critics believe that the faith movement is actually preaching "another Jesus" and that this error is more serious than any others in the movement's teaching. However, given the complexity of the issue and my own judgment that it is not central to my discussion of the movement, I have chosen not to discuss it at any length. For defense of this doctrine, see the works listed in chap. 4, note 7, and Paul Billheimer, *Destined for the Throne* (Ft. Washington, Pa.: Christian Literature Crusade, 1975—a book endorsed by Billy Graham), pp. 83-94; for the opposite view, see Onken, "The Atonement of Christ"; Judith Matta, *The Born-Again Jesus* (La Mirada, Calif.: Spirit of Truth Ministries, 1982); Swaggart, *Hyper-Faith*, pp. 35-38; David Alsobrook, *Was the Cross Enough?* (Paducah, Ky.: David Alsobrook Ministries, 1984); David Graybiel, "Destined for Whose Throne?" *CAI Newsletter*, Summer 1983, pp. 2-4, 14, 21-22.

Chapter 8

¹Capps, *Releasing the Ability*, pp. 13-14; Hagin, *Prevailing Prayer*, p. 81; Hagin, Jr., *Faith Worketh*, p. 3.

²For a few of the countless references to Proverbs 6:2 in faith literature, see Hagin, *Exceedingly*, pp. 78, 100; Kenneth Copeland, *The Power of the Tongue* (Fort Worth, Tex.: Kenneth Copeland Publications, 1980), p. 29; Capps, *The Tongue*, pp. 55, 90, 129; Price, *How Faith Works*, pp. 58, 116.

³Heb 3:1 or Heb 4:14 (a parallel passage) is cited by Osborn, *Healing the Sick*, p. 77; Capps, *The Tongue*, p. 88; Capps, *Releasing the Ability*, pp. 93-94; Hagin, *Right and Wrong Thinking*, p. 5; Hagin, *New Thresholds*, p. 16; Hagin, *In Him*, p. 3.

⁴Capps, *Releasing the Ability*, pp. 56-58.

⁵Kenneth Copeland, *Laws of Prosperity*, pp. 62-65; see also Price, *How Faith Works*, p. 27.

⁶Fee, *Disease*, p. 5 and Philip Lochhaas, "The Theology of Positive Confession from the Lutheran Perspective" (unpub., available from LC-MS), p. 4, have also discussed Copeland's interpretation of this passage. For an excellent discussion of the pitfalls of "The Lord told me" teaching styles, see Harold Bussell, *Unholy Devotion* (Grand Rapids, Mich.: Zondervan, 1983), pp. 29-40.

⁷Gloria Copeland, *God's Will for You*, p. 58.

⁸Tilton used Mt 18:19 in this way in two letters to people on his mailing list, in spring and summer 1985.

⁹Farah, "Critical Analysis," p. 15.

¹⁰Kenneth E. Hagin, *The Gift of Prophecy* (Tulsa, Okla.: Kenneth Hagin Ministries, 1969), pp. 24-25.

¹¹See, e.g., Hagin, *How You Can Be Led,* pp. 83-92, 108; Hagin, *Seven Steps to Judging Prophecy* (Tulsa, Okla.: Kenneth Hagin Ministries, 1982), p. 6.

¹²Gloria Copeland, *God's Will Is Prosperity,* p. 47; Kenneth Copeland, "The Gift of Righteousness," p. 4, and Gloria Copeland, "The Heart of Man," p. 5, both in *BVV,* October 1984.

¹³Hagin, *Believer's Authority,* p. 13.

¹⁴Hagin, *Name of Jesus,* p. 9.

¹⁵Catalog of materials distributed by Jerry Savelle Ministries (obtained by the author in spring 1985), p. 20. The visitation is described in Savelle, *Living in Divine Prosperity,* pp. 7-11.

¹⁶See, e.g., the sermon "How to Write Your Own Ticket with God" in *Exceedingly,* pp. 75-93; Hagin, *How God Taught Me about Prosperity.*

¹⁷This is question #19 in the Rhema Bible Correspondence Course test (Year 2, Lesson 5) on Capps's booklet *God's Creative Power Will Work for You.*

¹⁸Fee, *Disease,* pp. 3, 13. The most complete compilation of questionable Bible interpretations is in the appendix to John Fickett, *Confess It, Possess It: Reflections on Faith-Formula Theology* (Oklahoma City, Okla.: Presbyterian and Reformed Renewal Ministries, 1984).

Chapter 9

¹Hagin, *I Believe,* pp. 13-14.

²While I feel the data I have accumulated are sufficient to justify these statements, no large-scale survey of faith churches has been done.

³It has been suggested to me that alternative (2), that God works differently with different people, actually contradicts faith theology. With regard to the faith teachers' most extreme statements, this may be true; however, I contend that the faith teachings on the whole leave room for moderation. For example, two researchers have told me that they have seen television programs in which Kenneth Hagin, in discussing reasons why some are not healed, showed more moderation than we might expect from reading his books.

⁴See Joni Eareckson with Joe Musser, *Joni* (Grand Rapids, Mich.: Zondervan, 1976).

⁵Eareckson, *A Step Further,* pp. 122-26. Joni told me in April 1986 that, eight years after the publication of *A Step Further,* she continued to receive about two dozen letters a week encouraging her to seek healing.

⁶Debby Zook, *Debby* (Scottdale, Pa.: Herald Press, 1974), pp. 124-25.

⁷I am indirectly indebted for this insight to John Lofland, *Doomsday Cult: A*

Study of Conversion, Proselytization, and Maintenance of Faith, enlgd. ed. (New York: Irvington, 1981), who similarly explains how members of the Unification Church can hold their seemingly untenable world view.

[8]Hagin, Jr., calls clearly for compassion in *Faith Worketh by Love,* and Capps reproaches those who look down on people who take medicine (*The Tongue,* p. 49), but I am not aware of any passage in faith literature that specifically addresses the problem of how to care for the terminally ill and dying.

[9]Swaggart, *Balanced Faith Life,* pp. 48-52.

[10]Ibid., p. 49.

[11]Larry Parker, *We Let Our Son Die* (Eugene, Oreg.: Harvest House, 1980); the Parkers' case is summarized, with penetrating theological reflection, in Steve Board, "Is Faith a High-Wire Act?" *Eternity,* July-August 1981, pp. 13-16, 26.

[12]Farah, "Critical Analysis," p. 20.

[13]Price, *Faith, Foolishness,* p. 117.

[14]Swaggart, *Balanced Faith Life,* pp. 4-5.

[15]Kenneth Copeland, "My Instructions," pp. 2-3.

[16]Hagin, Jr., *Get Acquainted,* pp. 7-9.

[17]Os Guinness, *The Gravedigger File* (Downers Grove, Ill.: InterVarsity Press, 1983), p. 133.

[18]Price, *How Faith Works,* pp. 28-29; see also Strang, "Ever Increasing Faith," pp. 20, 23.

[19]*CAI Newsletter,* Summer 1983, pp. 18-19, reprinted from *CharisLife,* July-August 1982.

[20]A few examples: Hagin's four steps on how to train the human spirit appear in *New Thresholds* (pp. 93-95), *How You Can Be Led* (pp. 127-37), and *Exceedingly* (pp. 59-71); he tells of his 1934 healing in several books; he and others cite Is 53, 1 Pet 2:24 and Mt 8:17 dozens of times.

[21]Hagin, Jr., *Itching Ears,* p. 20.

[22]The source for the following story is Ben Byrd, taped letter to author, 9 August 1985.

[23]Savelle, *Living in Divine Prosperity,* pp. 215-54 (esp. pp. 251-54) covers the same topic and corroborates what Byrd recalls of the message's content.

[24]David Wilkerson also cites Rev 3:17 as a condemnation of "peace and prosperity" preachers, in *Set the Trumpet to Thy Mouth* (Lindale, Tex.: World Challenge, 1985), pp. 144-45.

Chapter 10

[1]Hagin refers to the Holy Spirit as teacher of John Alexander Dowie, whose work predated the Pentecostal movement, in his tape "Abraham's Blessing," available from SLW. He also cites the non-Pentecostal Charles G. Finney as the greatest evangelist since the apostle Paul, in *The Interceding Christian* (Tulsa, Okla.: Kenneth Hagin Ministries, 1983), p. 26. On shepherding abuses, see Jerram Barrs, *Shepherds and Sheep* (Downers Grove, Ill.: InterVar-

sity Press, 1983); Barron, *If You Really;* Bill Ligon, *Discipleship: The Jesus View* (Plainfield, N.J.: Logos, 1979).

2Donald L. Clark, "An Implicit Theory of Personality, Illness, and Cure Found in the Writings of Neo-Pentecostal Faith Teachers," *Journal of Psychology and Theology* 12 (4):284 (1984).

3See the book of Jude and the first chapter of Job for the most striking examples.

4Naturally the faith teachers are not the first people to whom has occurred the idea of bringing Satan colorfully to life for purposes of Christian instruction. They are in good company. Perhaps their greatest predecessor is C. S. Lewis who wrote *The Screwtape Letters* (New York: Macmillan, 1959).

5Dietrich Bonhoeffer, *The Cost of Discipleship,* trans. R. H. Fuller (New York: Macmillan, 1949), pp. 37-49.

6I am convinced that there is a direct correlation between irresponsible biblical interpretation and schism within the Christian church. Could the "Jesus only" movement, for example—a branch of Pentecostalism which dogmatically rejects the Trinity on the basis of a few proof texts—ever have been born in an evangelical seminary? See Anderson, *Vision,* chaps. 9-10; Synan, *Holiness-Pentecostal Movement,* pp. 147-53; David Reed, "Aspects of the Origins of Oneness Pentecostalism," in Vinson Synan, ed., *Aspects of Pentecostal-Charismatic Origins* (Plainfield, N.J.: Logos, 1975), pp. 145-68, esp. pp. 154-57.

7On Dowie's claim to be Elijah, see Harrell, *All Things,* p. 14; on Paul's situation see 2 Tim 2:17-18.

8The cases of Charles Taze Russell and Joseph Smith, founders of the Jehovah's Witnesses and the Mormons respectively, are classic examples of men who listened to no one and gave birth to theological cultism. See, e.g., James Bjornstad, *Counterfeits at Your Door* (Ventura, Calif.: Regal, 1979), pp. 59, 101. See also our discussion of Hobart Freeman (chap. 2) and the results of isolation and refusal to listen to other Christians.

9Every Christian should read at least one good book on hermeneutics such as Gordon Fee and Douglas Stuart, *How to Read the Bible for All Its Worth* (Grand Rapids, Mich.: Zondervan, 1982), or James Sire, *Scripture Twisting: Twenty Ways the Cults Misread the Bible* (Downers Grove, Ill.: InterVarsity Press, 1980).

10Dennis Bennett, *Moving Right Along in the Spirit* (Old Tappan, N.J.: Revell, 1983), pp. 113, 95, 105.

11Ibid., p. 111.

12Ibid., pp. 97-100, 117-18.

13MacNutt, *Healing,* pp. 102-5, 124-25.

14Ibid., pp. 186-87, 227, 236, 132.

15Ibid., p. 107, crediting the statement to Dr. Bogart Van Dunne.

16Culpepper, *Evaluating the Charismatic Movement,* p. 125.

[17]An excellent recent treatment of healing in all its forms is Richard Sipley, *Understanding Divine Healing* (Wheaton, Ill.: Victor, 1986). See also Roy Lawrence, *Christian Healing Rediscovered* (Downers Grove, Ill.: InterVarsity Press, 1980).

[18]Price, *Faith, Foolishness,* p. 34.

[19]The image comes from a scene early in the movie version of *The Cross and the Switchblade,* in which David Wilkerson (played by Pat Boone), when told that he is too well dressed to relate to ghetto youth, takes off his shoes and walks through the streets in stocking feet.

[20]For example, one man who worked at the community run by the late Keith Green, a Christian musician and evangelist, later commented, "Keith is a confusing and intense person. I cannot remember any time when he was really joyful or loving." Material available from CFF national office.

[21]Rom 8:28, 37; Phil 4:13.

[22]Phil 4:4; 1 Thess 5:16-18; Acts 5:41, 16:25; Jas 1:2.

[23]See Capps, *The Tongue,* pp. 146-47, for an example of the attitude of "don't pray the problem." On the fourth point, it must be added that Psalm 88, not written by David, is an enigmatic exception to this principle. Perhaps its concluding despair is meant to suggest that some sadness in this world is too deep to be resolved in the time period covered by a single poem. Job's friends felt a need to sit with him silently for a week before they said anything. I am also reminded of my friend who, when asked how to deal with a post-Holocaust Jew questioning whether life and God have any meaning, said, "The first thing to do is to sit and cry with him for a while."

[24]The ad hoc committee's report was made public on 8 May 1984, Maranatha's response on 9 August 1984. See also John J. Fialka, "Maranatha Christians, Backing Rightist Ideas, Draw Fire over Tactics," *Wall Street Journal,* 16 August 1985.

[25]Derek Prince, long a leader in the authoritarian shepherding movement, changed his theology in 1984; see his tapes "Plurality and Balance" and "Absolutes and Variables" (Ft. Lauderdale, Fla.: Derek Prince Ministries, 1984). Keith Green similarly repented of abuses of authority at his ministry's headquarters; see his letter of 17 February 1981 and letters from former workers, both available from the CFF national office.

[26]E.g., Ron and Judy House, *Hyper-Faith Charges Examined* (Jacksonville, Fla.: Living Word Ministries, 1982), p. 7. This is an article written by a faith pastor couple in Florida in response to Jimmy Swaggart. I have received similar comments from other faith people.

[27]Charles Farah, Jr., letter to author, 26 September 1983.

[28]Strang, "Robert Tilton," p. 26.

[29]Farah tells of the faith teachers' unwillingness to enter dialog in "Critical Analysis," p. 17.

[30]Onken, in "The Atonement of Christ," p. 15, argued that the faith message

was bound to move into more serious error, but actually recent articles (especially in *BVV* since 1985) suggest that the faith movement may be paying more attention to intercession, love and care for the poor.

Topical Index

Scripture Index